jazz pop

Arranged by Brent Edstrom

ISBN 978-1-4234-5913-2

7777 W. BLUEMOUND RD. P.O. BOX 13819 MILWAUKEE, WI 53213

Visit Hal Leonard Online at
www.halleonard.com

contents

FIELDS OF GOLD

Music and Lyrics by
STING

Flowing

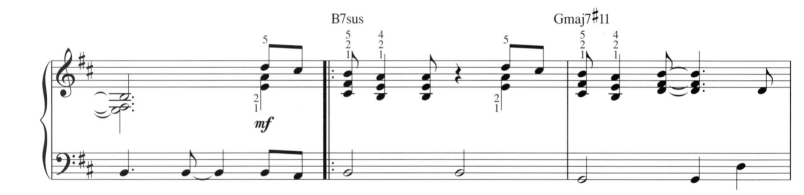

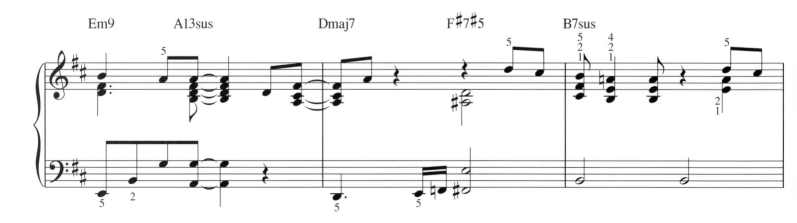

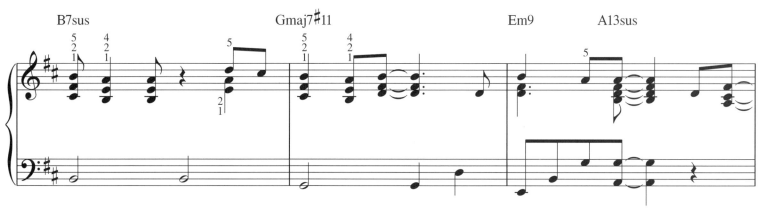

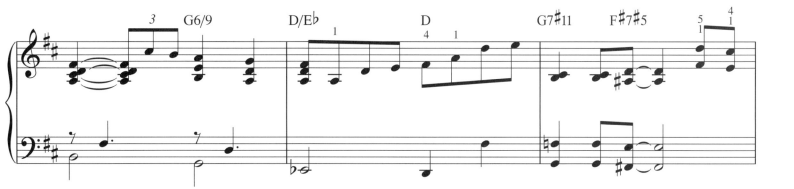

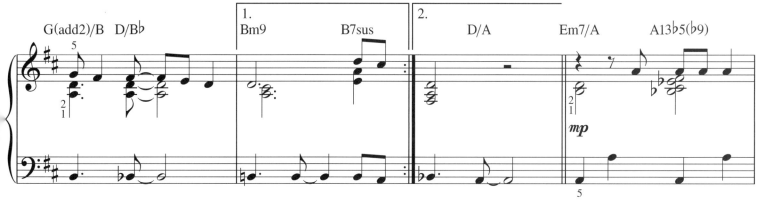

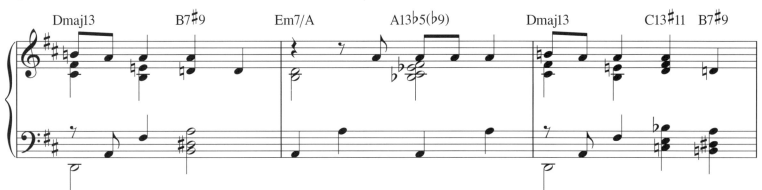

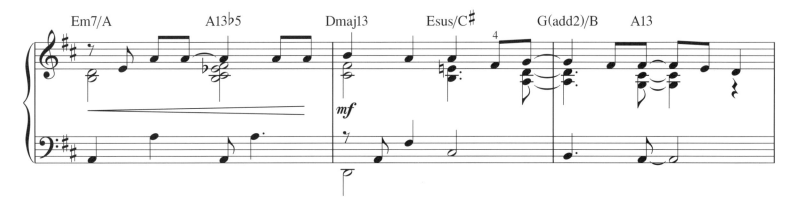

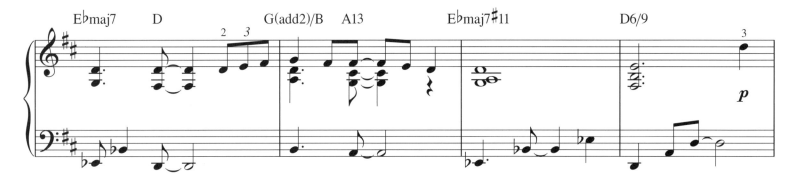

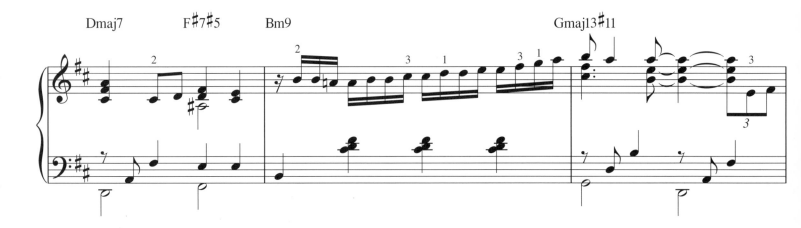

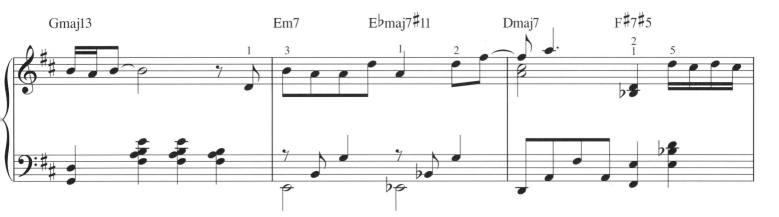

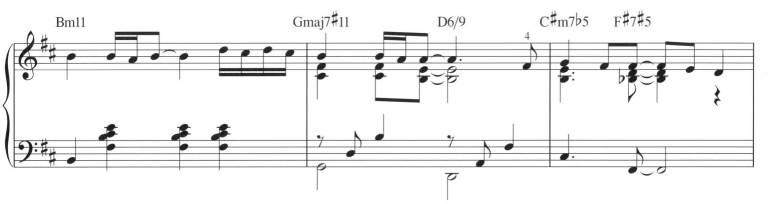

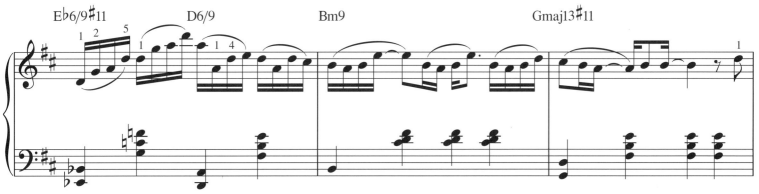

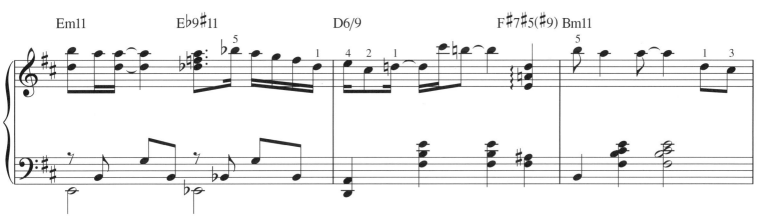

AGAINST ALL ODDS
(Take a Look at Me Now)
from AGAINST ALL ODDS

Words and Music by
PHIL COLLINS

Moderately slow

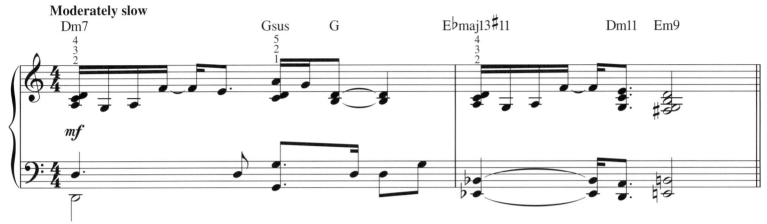

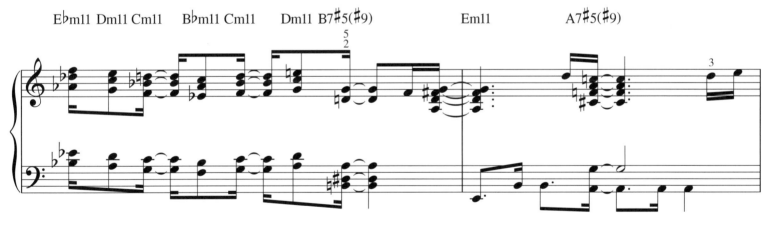

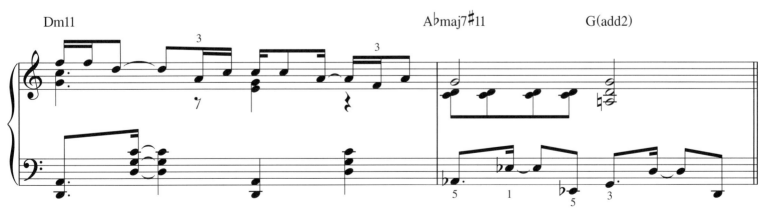

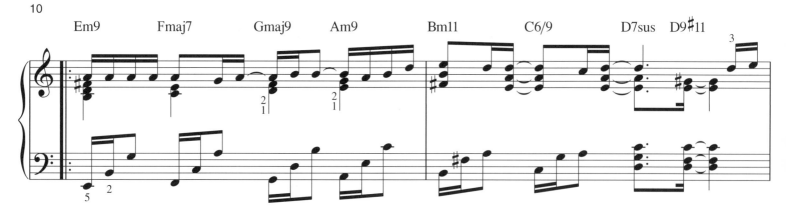

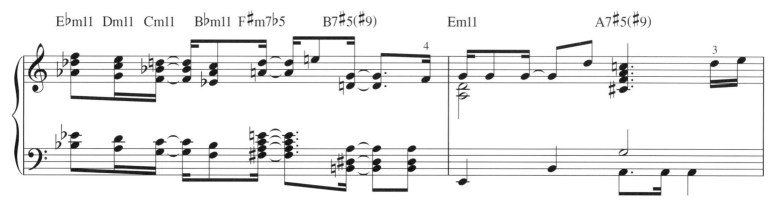

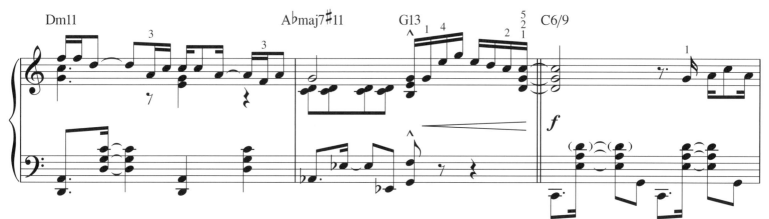

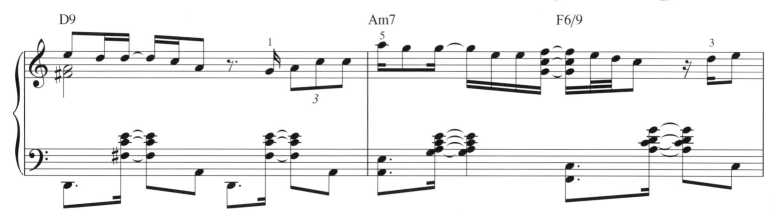

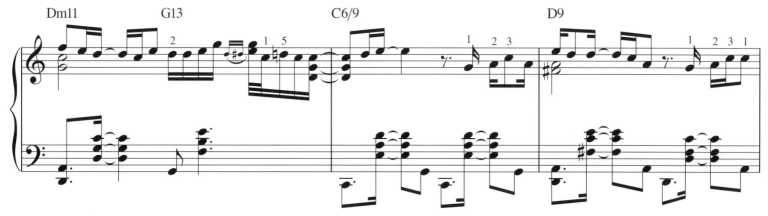

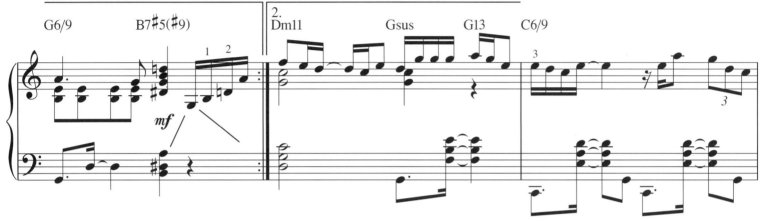

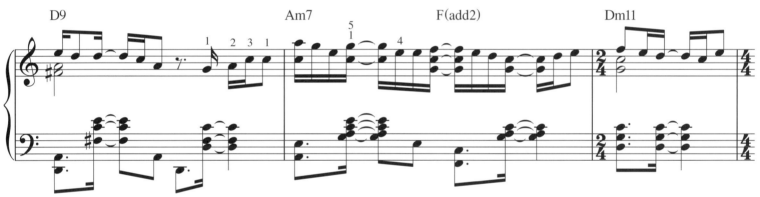

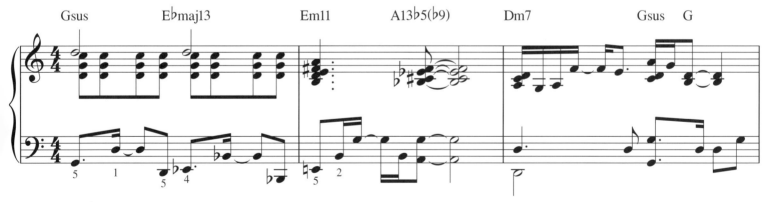

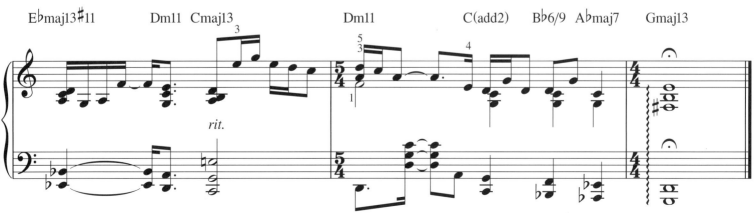

BLACKBIRD

Words and Music by JOHN LENNON
and PAUL McCARTNEY

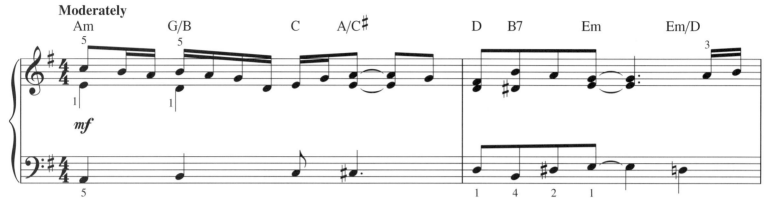

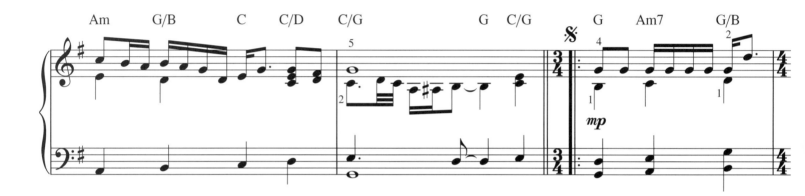

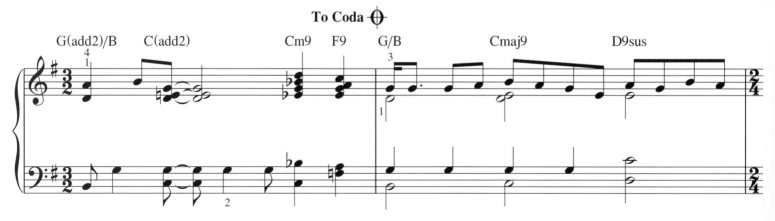

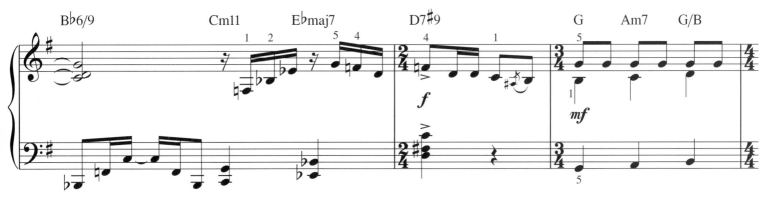

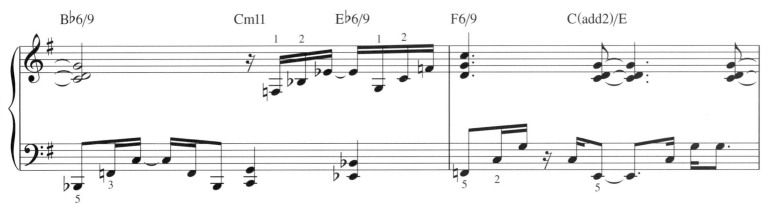

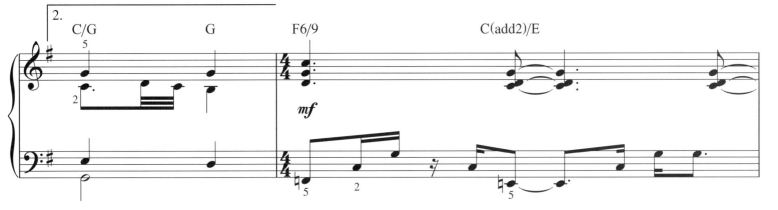

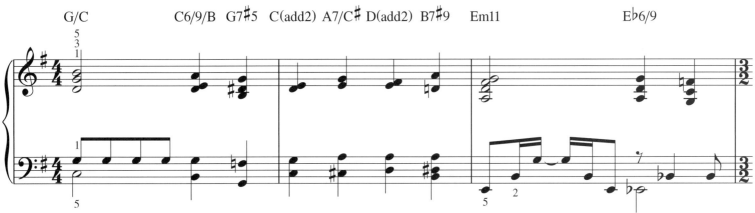

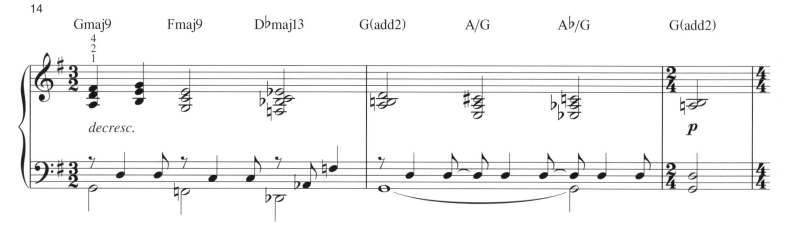

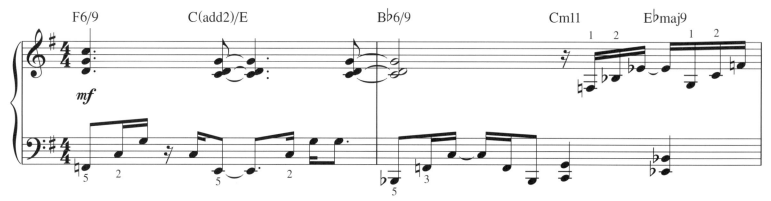

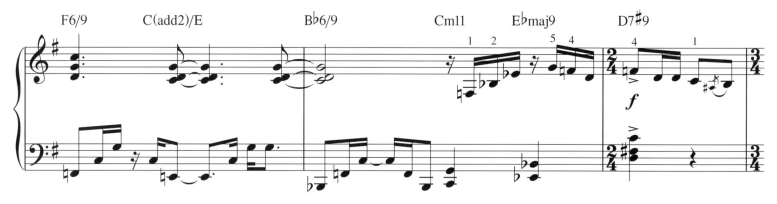

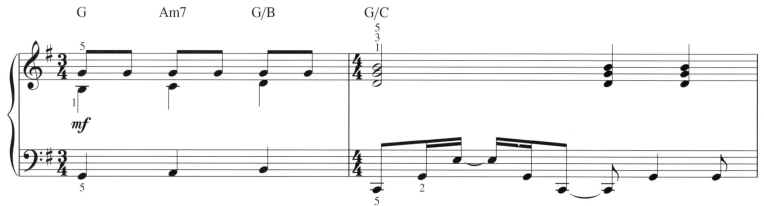

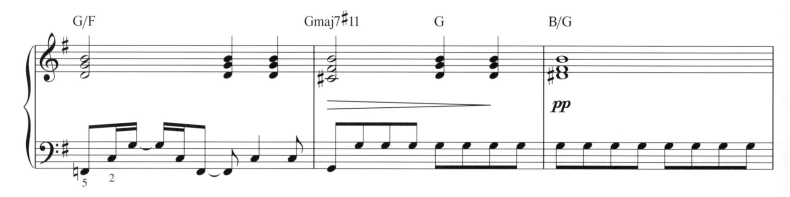

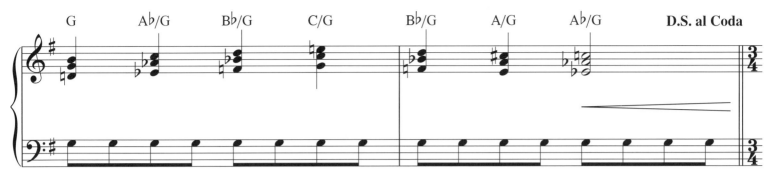

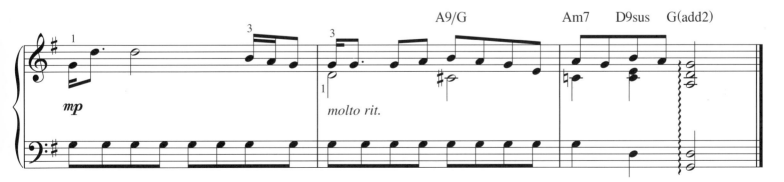

DON'T KNOW WHY

Words and Music by
JESSE HARRIS

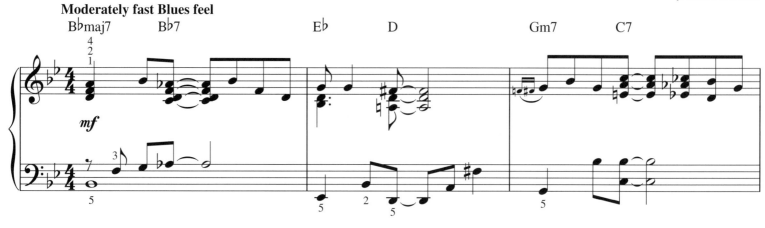

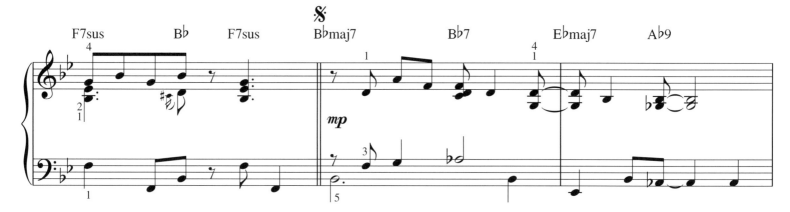

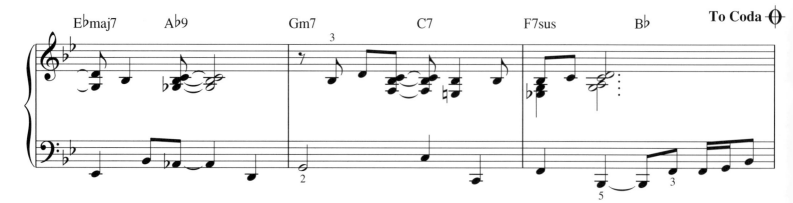

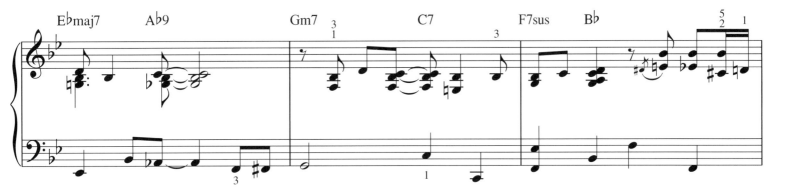

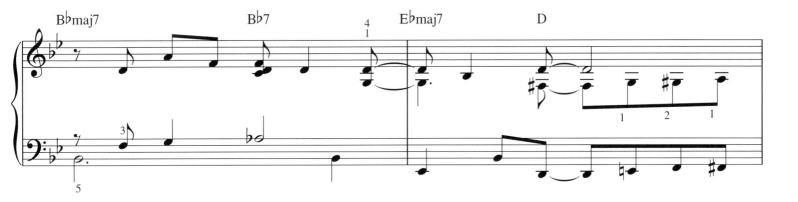

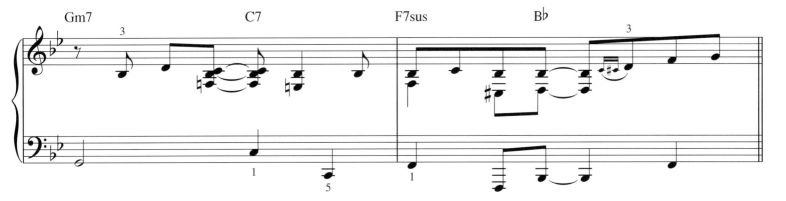

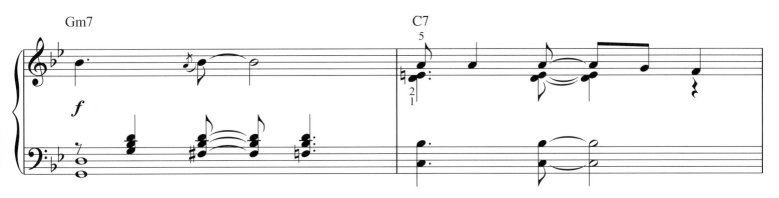

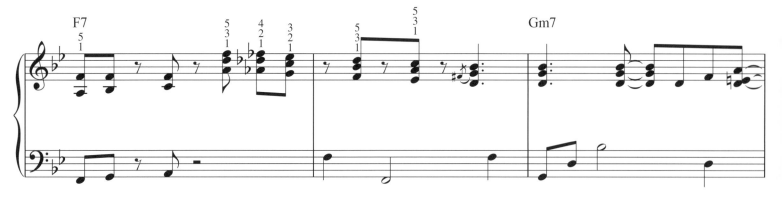

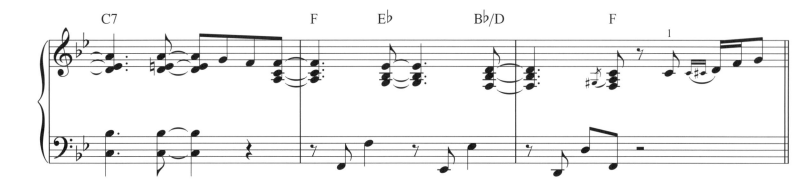

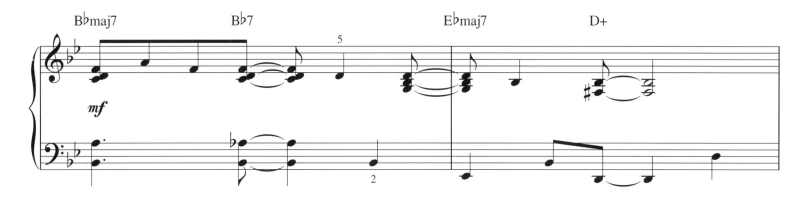

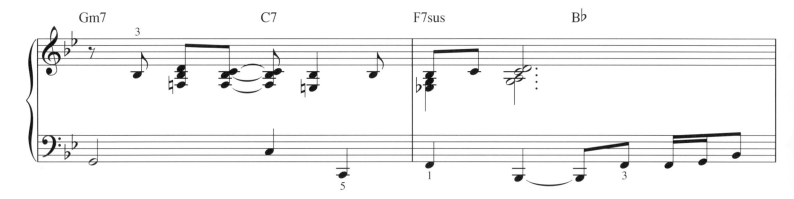

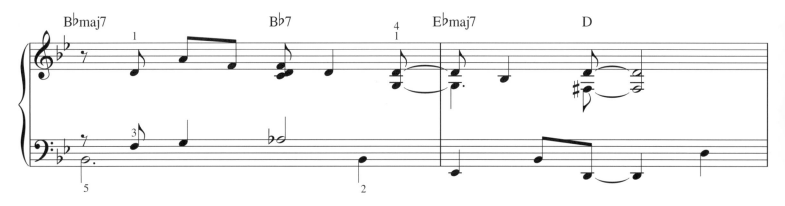

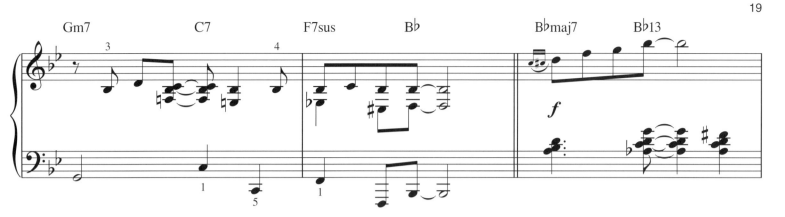

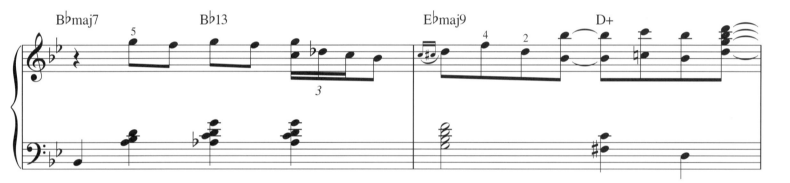

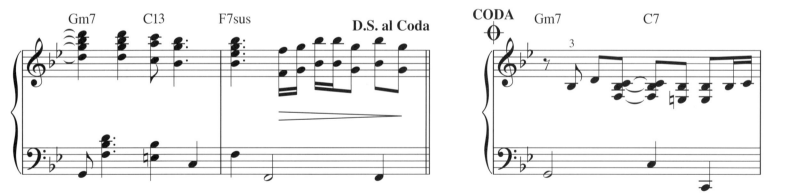

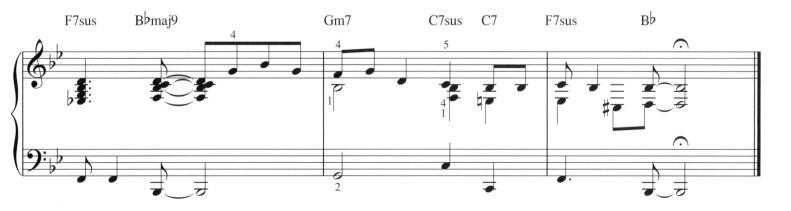

I JUST CALLED TO SAY I LOVE YOU

Words and Music by
STEVIE WONDER

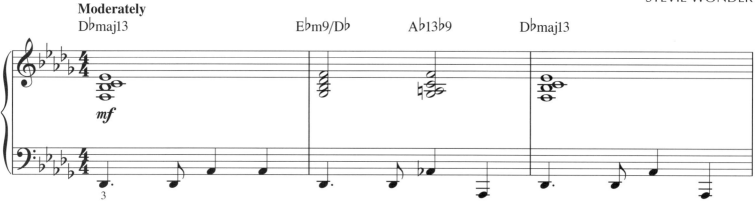

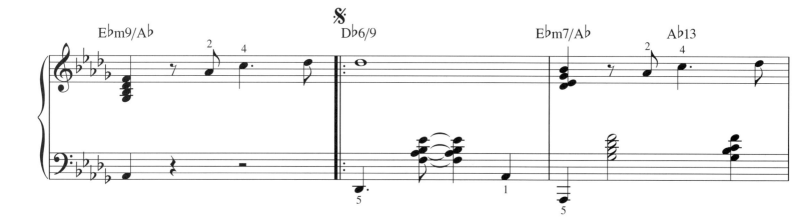

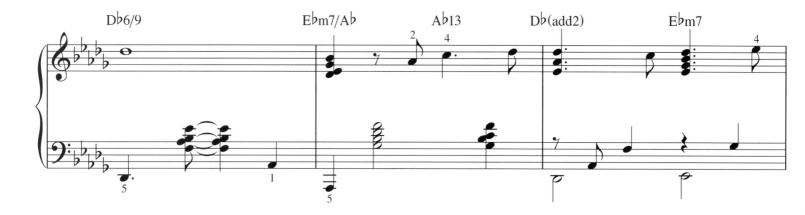

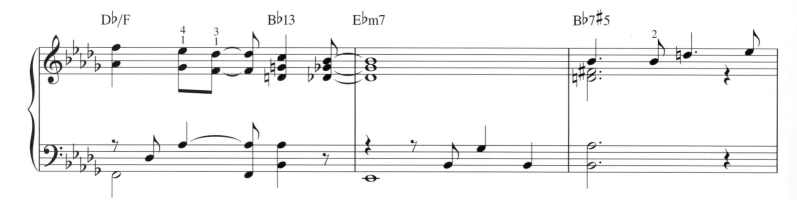

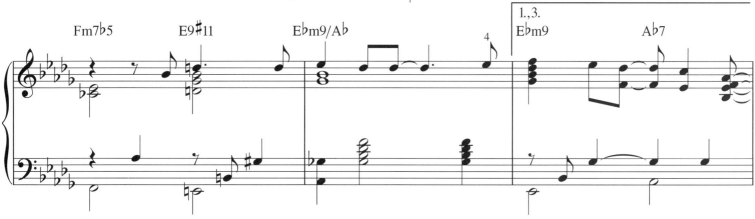

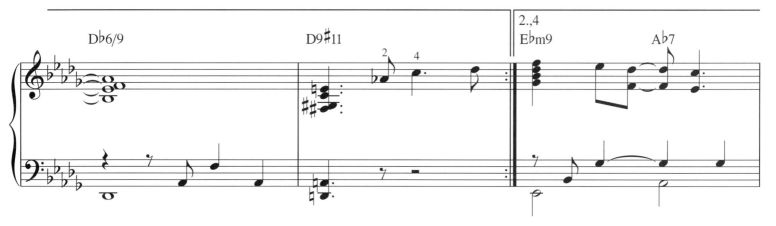

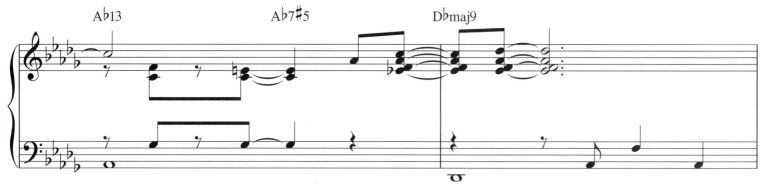

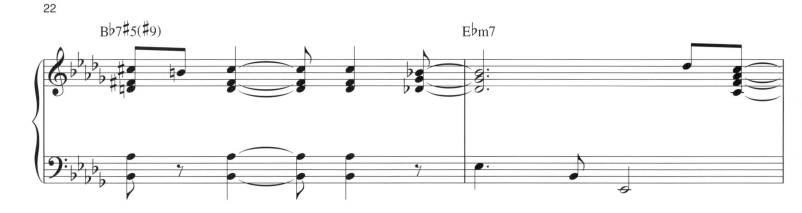

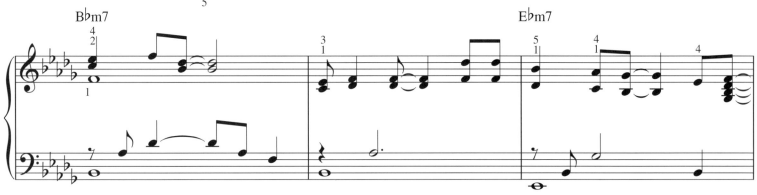

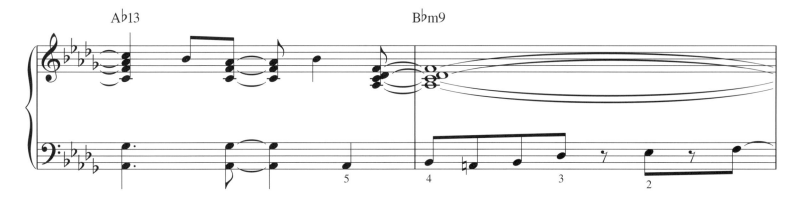

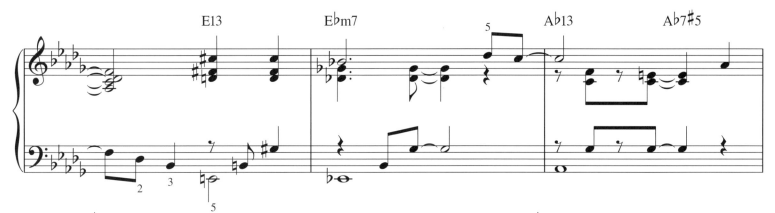

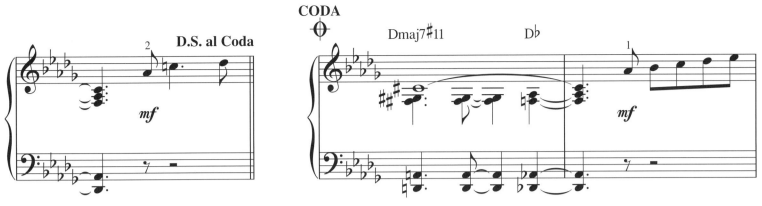

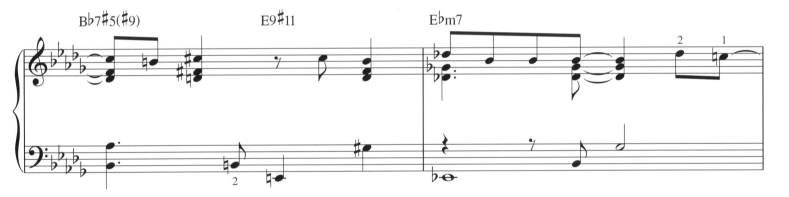

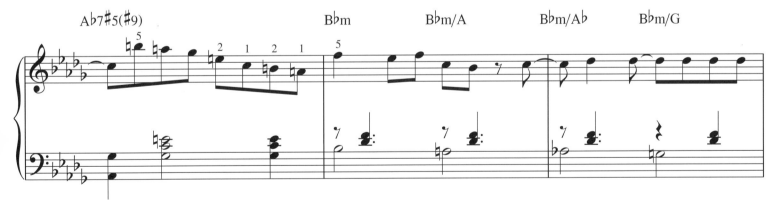

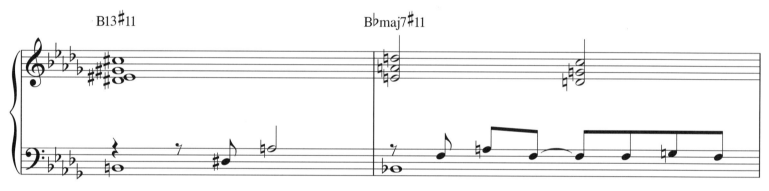

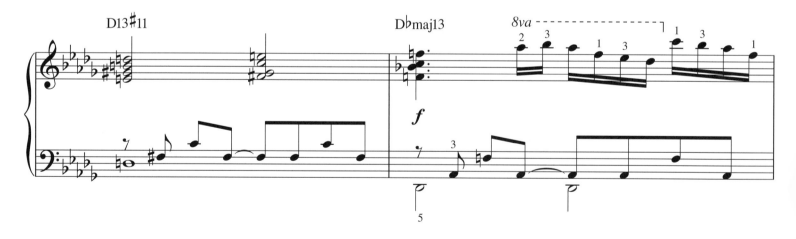

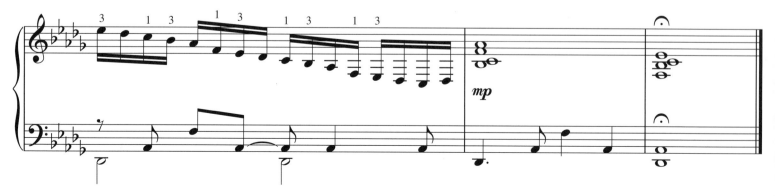

IF YOU LEAVE ME NOW

Words and Music by
PETER CETERA

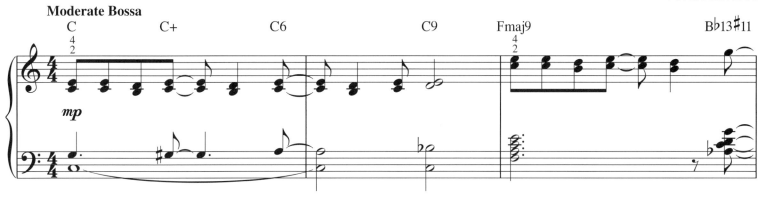

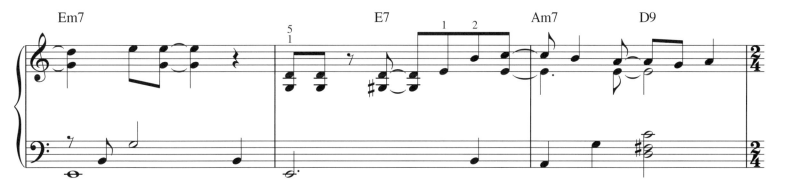

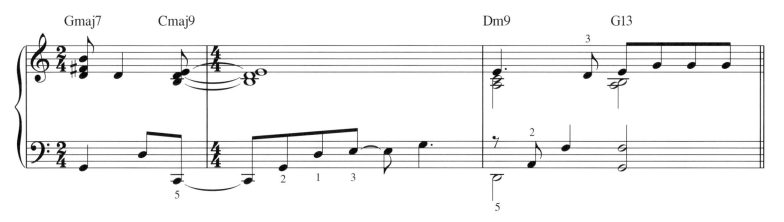

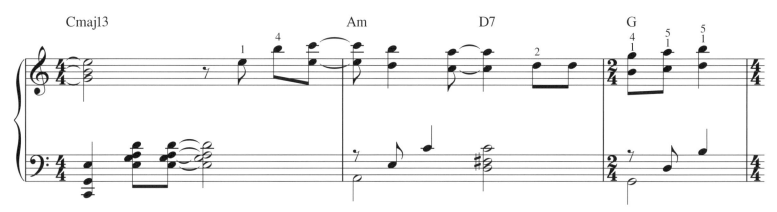

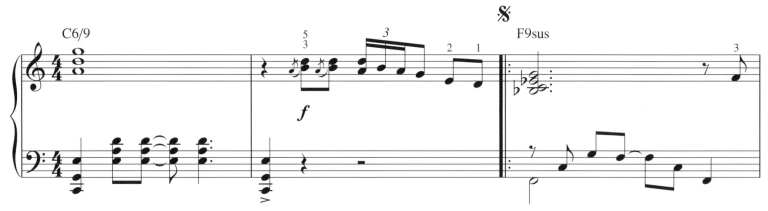

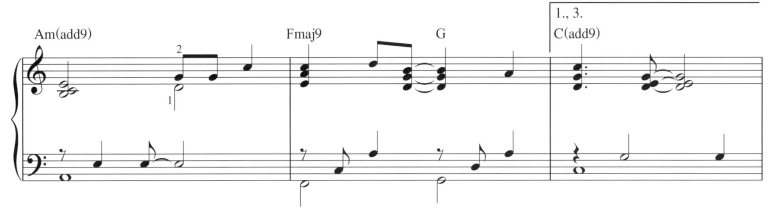

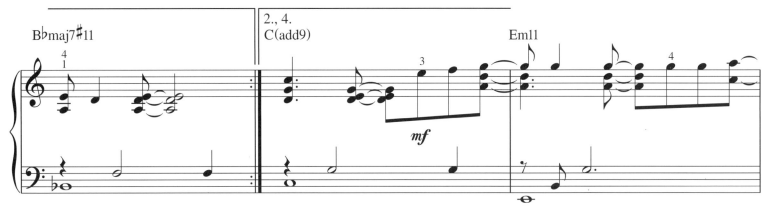

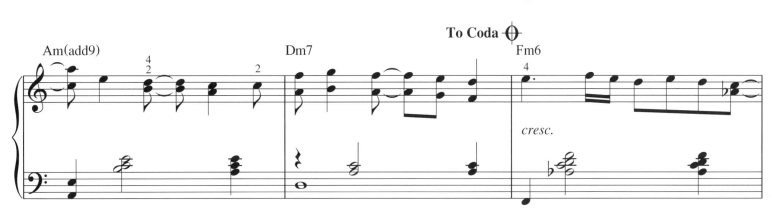

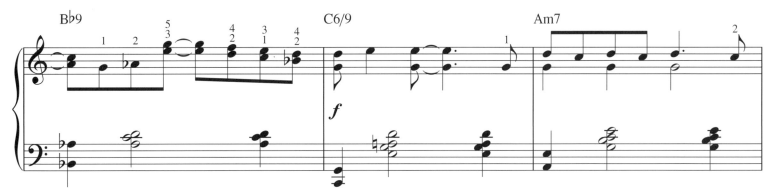

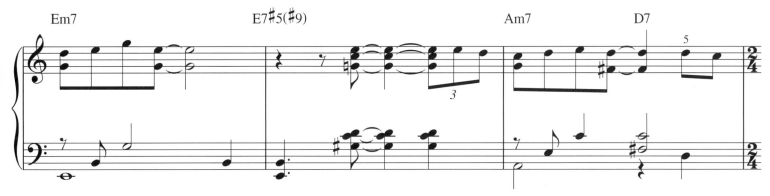

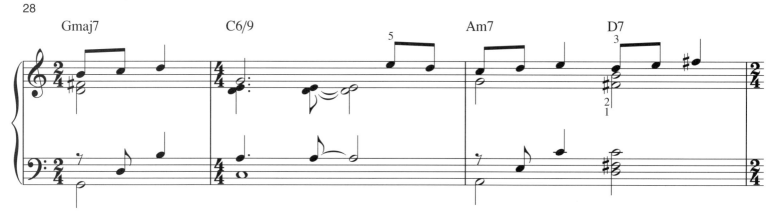

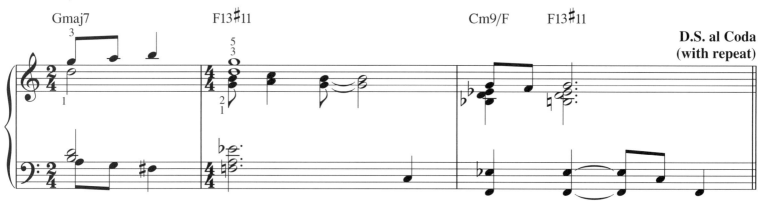

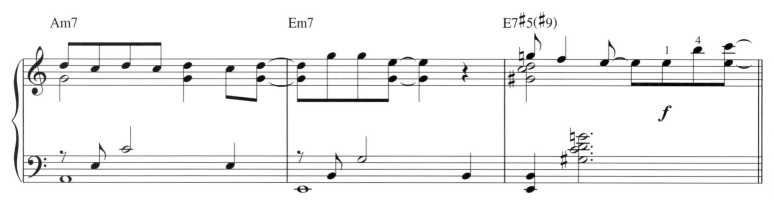

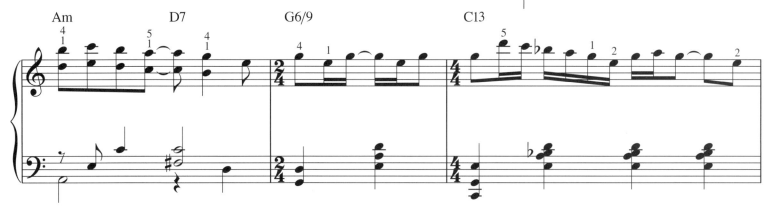

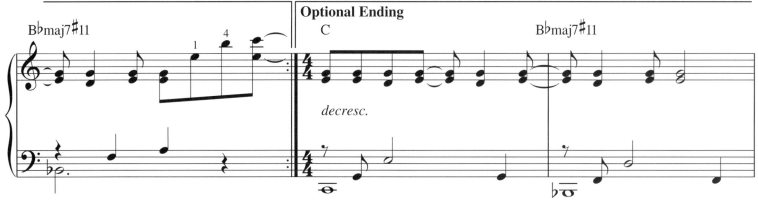

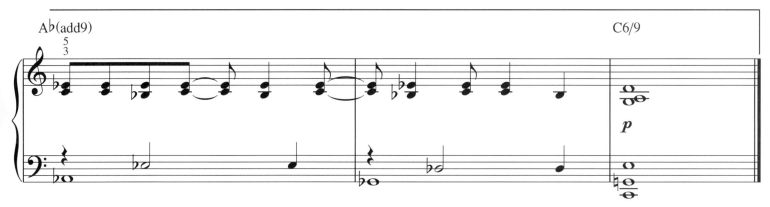

I SHOT THE SHERIFF

Words and Music by
BOB MARLEY

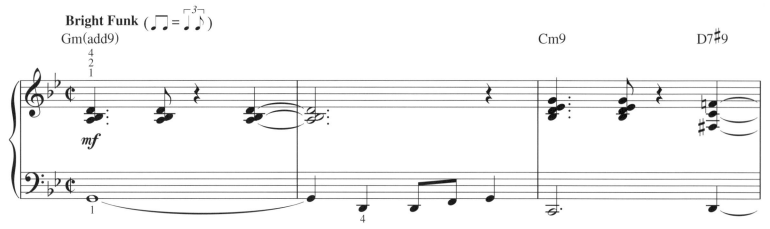

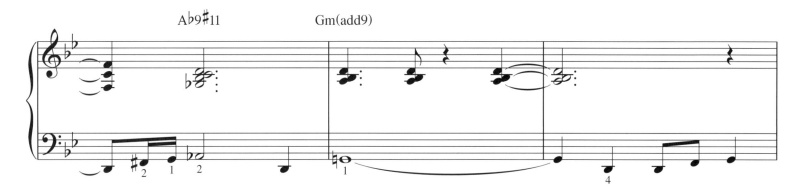

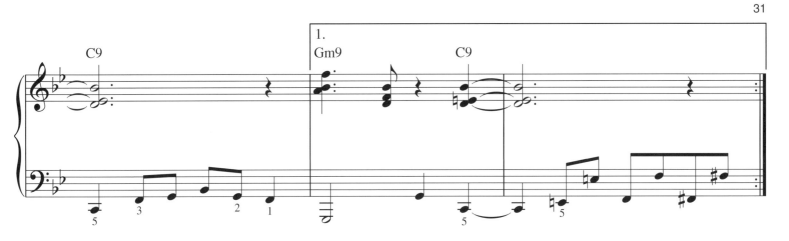

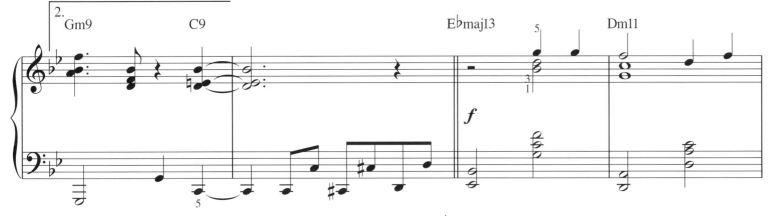

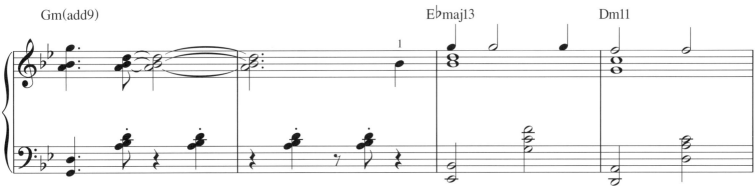

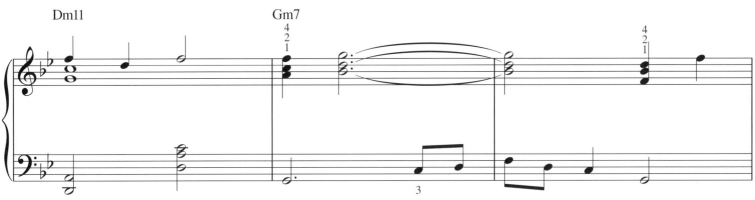

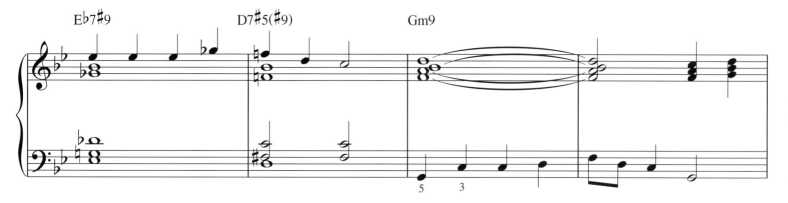

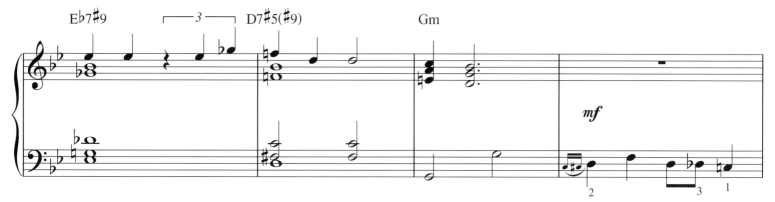

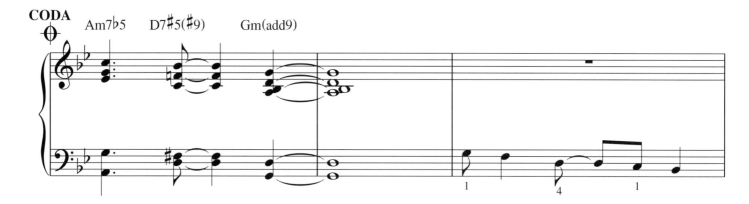

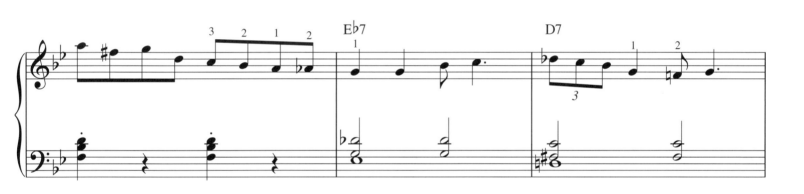

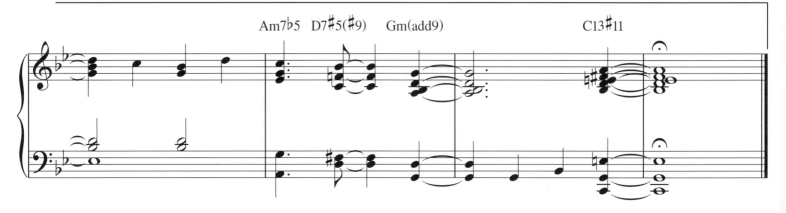

IT'S TOO LATE

Words and Music by CAROLE KING
and TONI STERN

Medium Latin

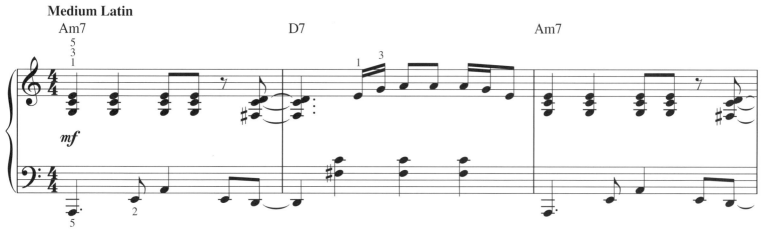

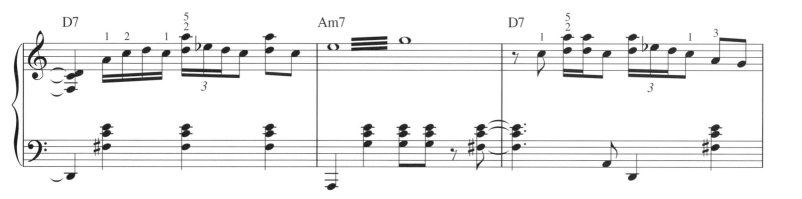

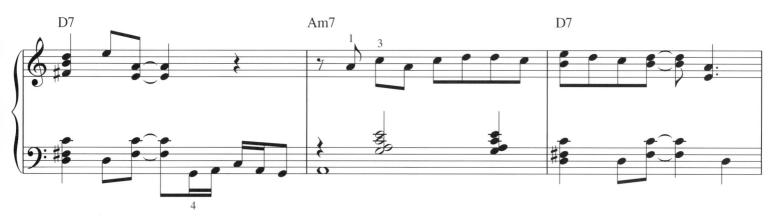

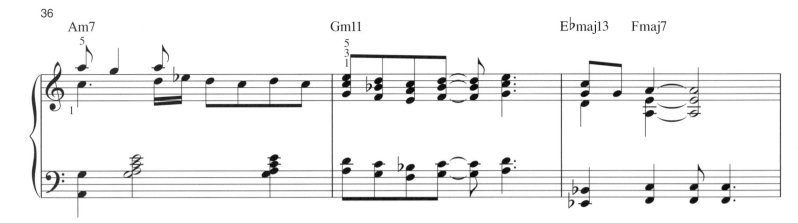

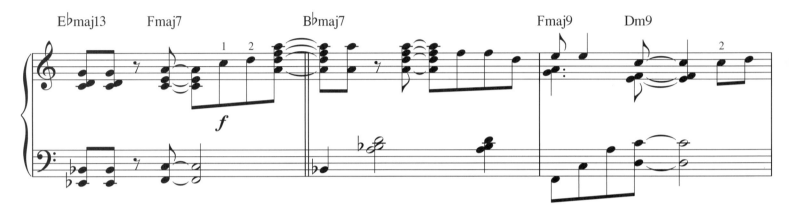

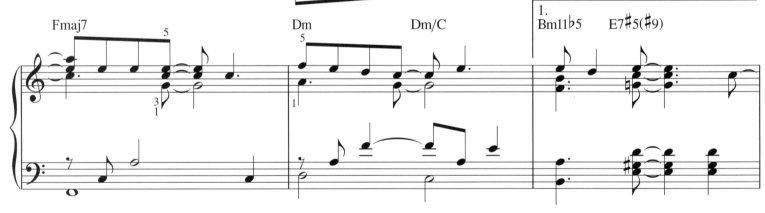

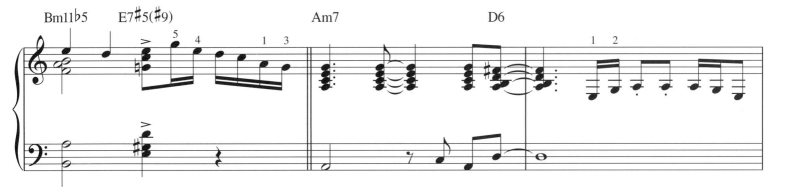

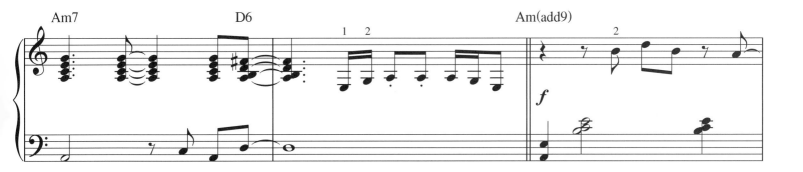

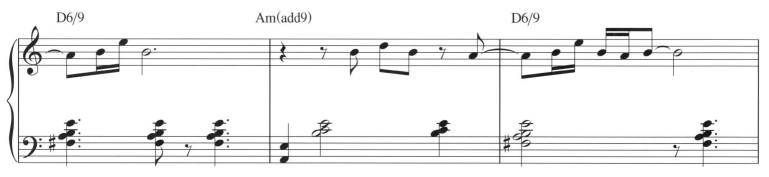

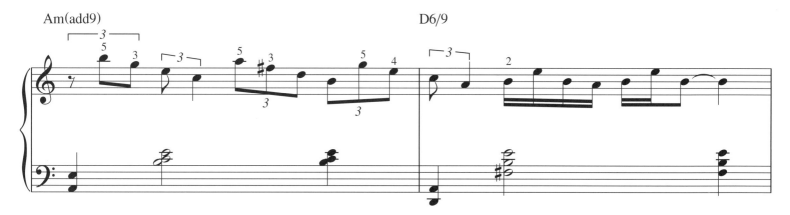

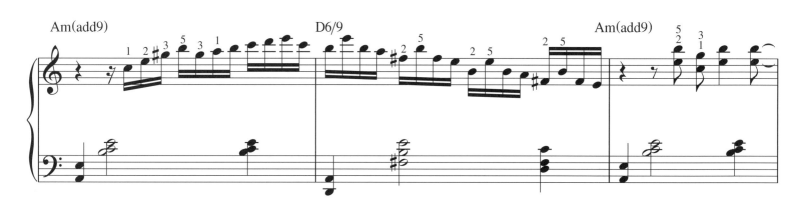

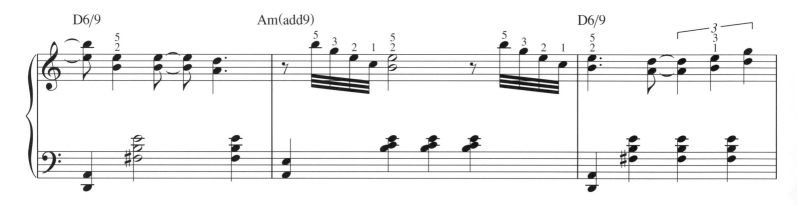

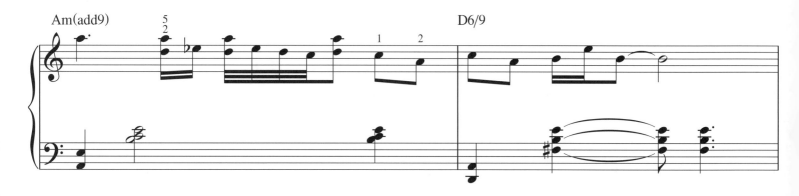

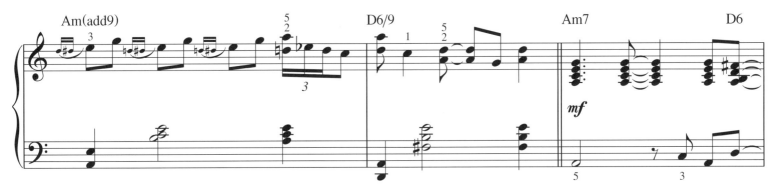

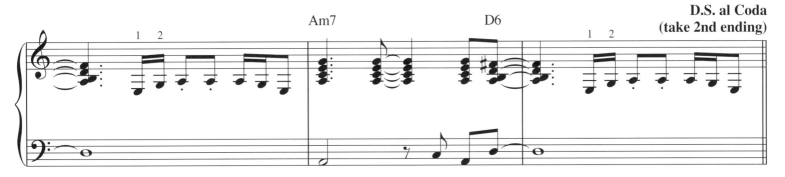

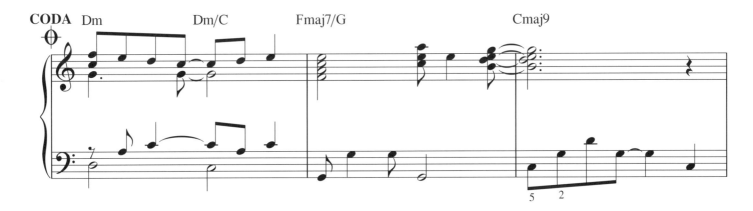

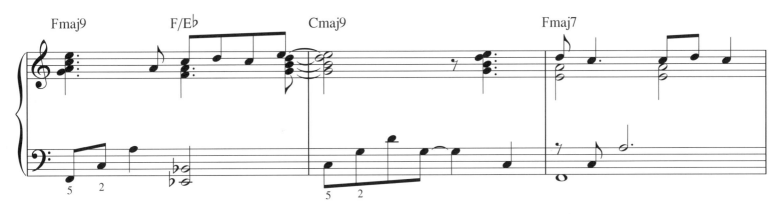

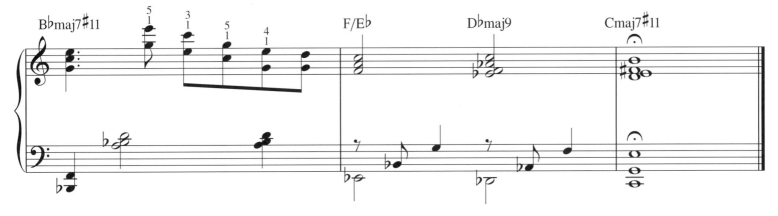

ISN'T SHE LOVELY

Words and Music by
STEVIE WONDER

Medium Swing

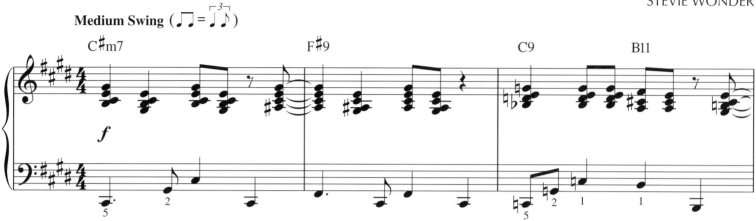

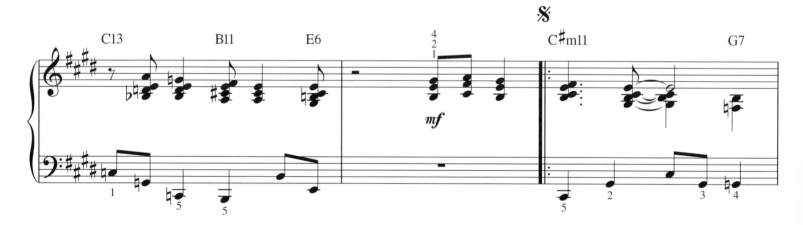

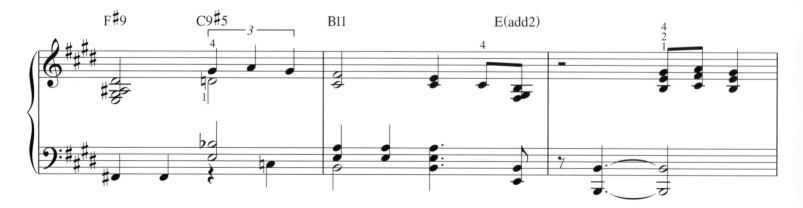

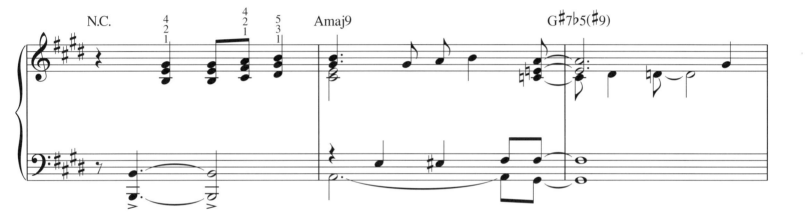

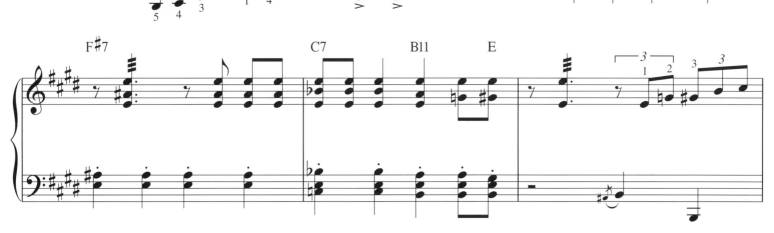

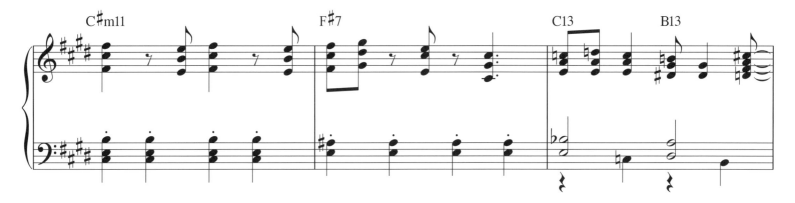

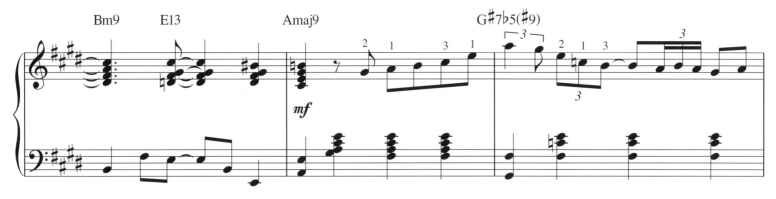

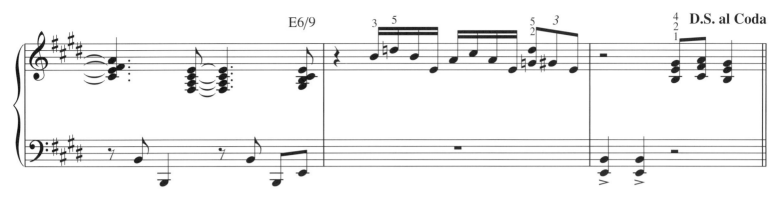

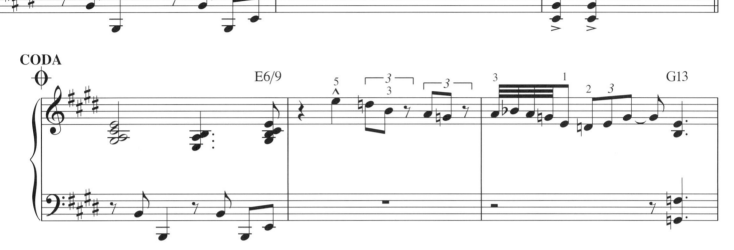

KILLING ME SOFTLY WITH HIS SONG

Words by NORMAN GIMBEL
Music by CHARLES FOX

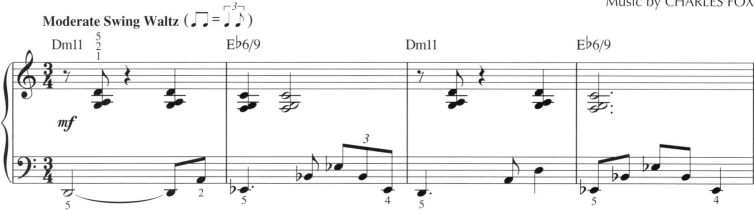

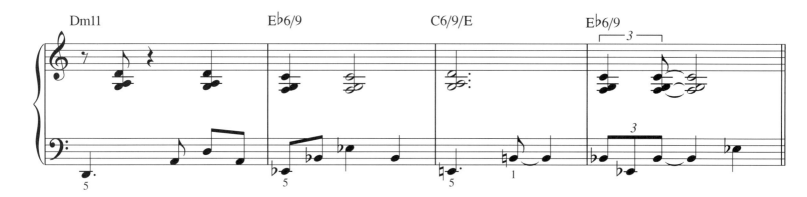

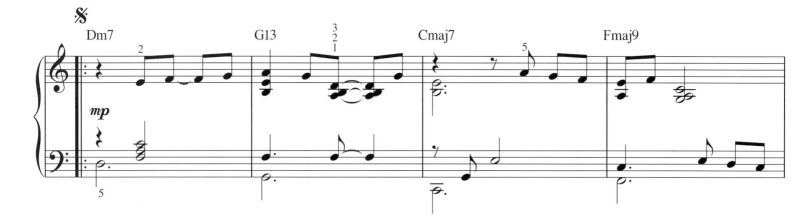

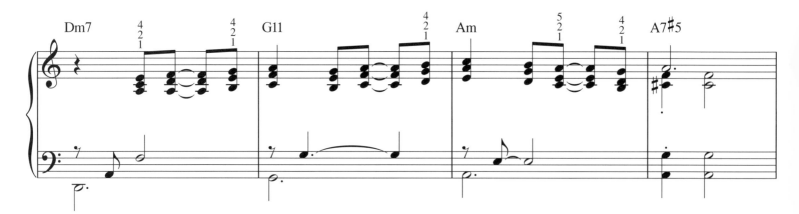

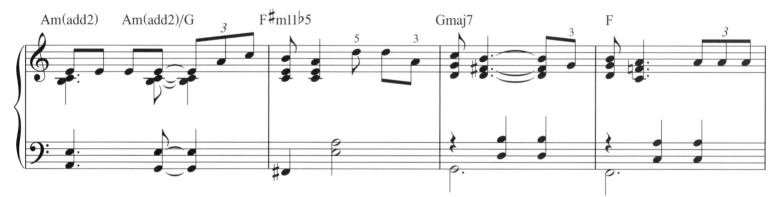

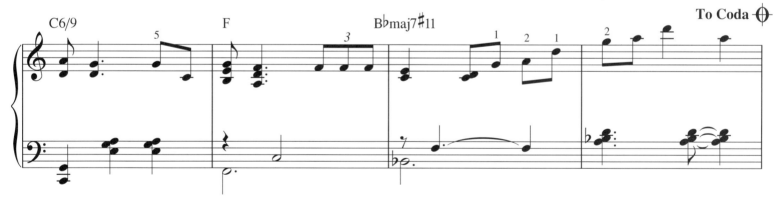

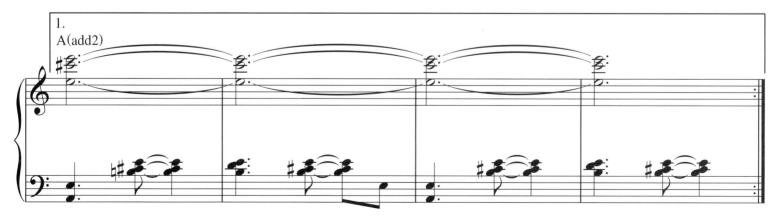

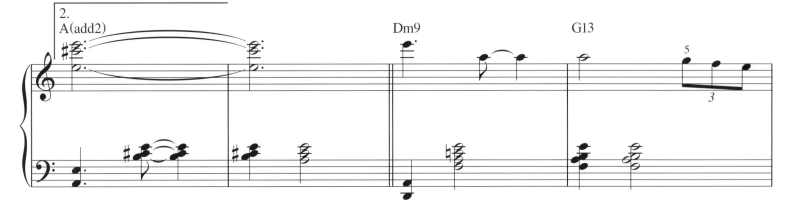

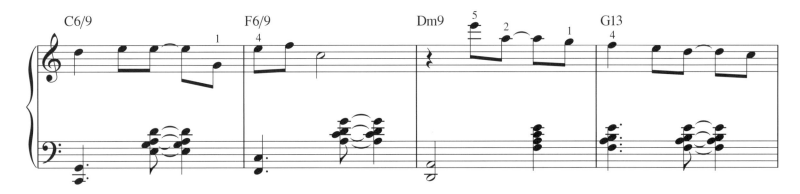

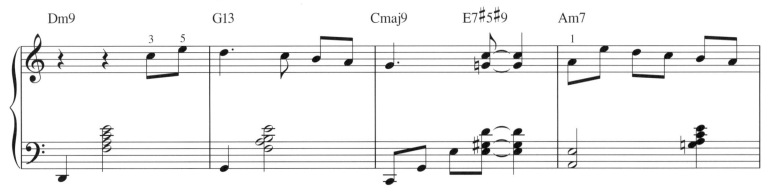

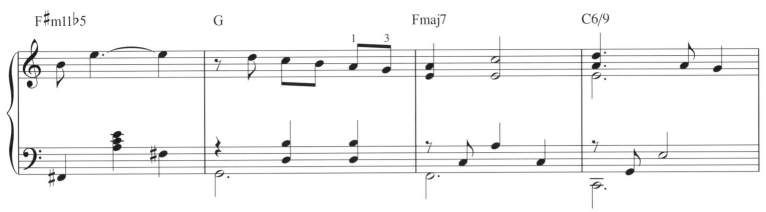

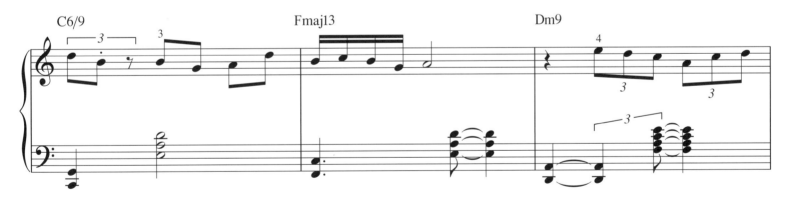

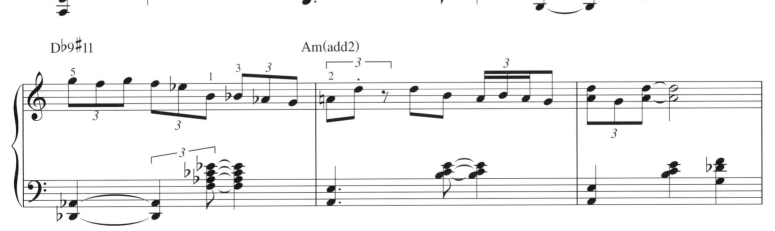

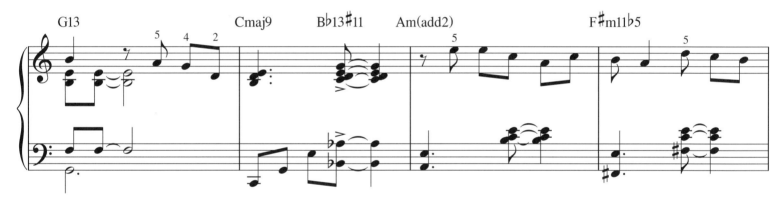

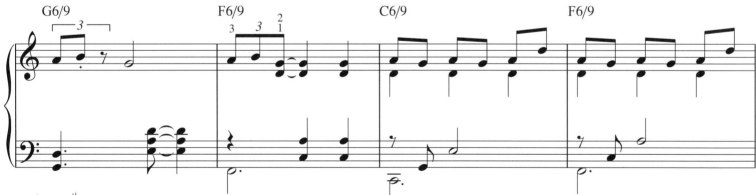

D.S. al Coda

CODA   A6/9

cresc.   *ff*

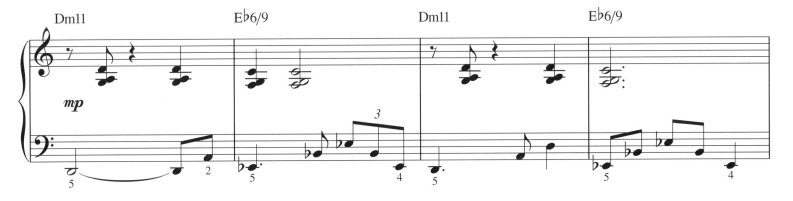

Dm11   Eb6/9   Dm11   Eb6/9

mp

Dm11   Eb6/9   C6/9/E   F6/9

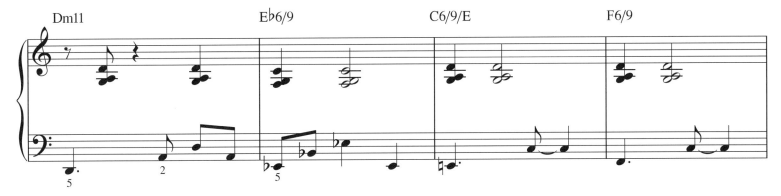

G(add2)   G6/9   A(add2)

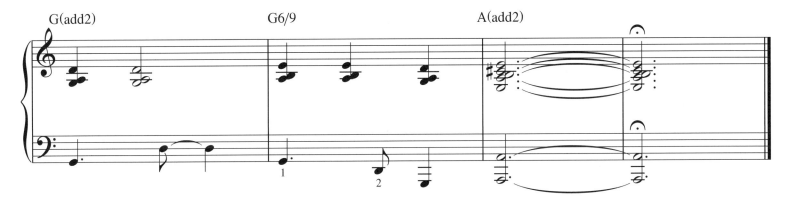

NEW YORK STATE OF MIND

Words and Music by
BILLY JOEL

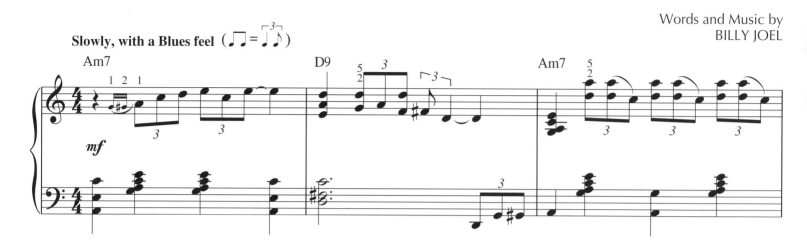

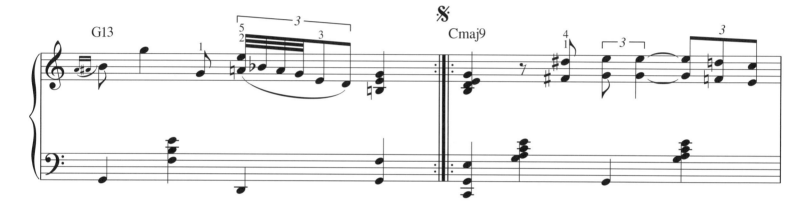

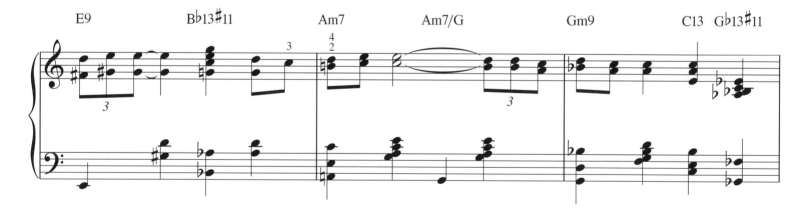

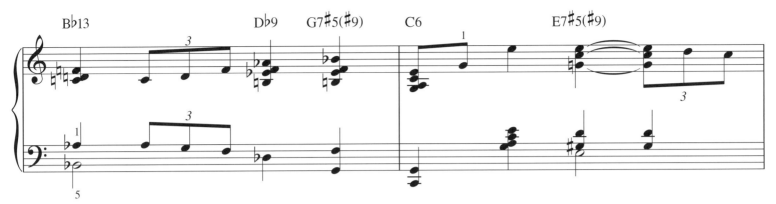

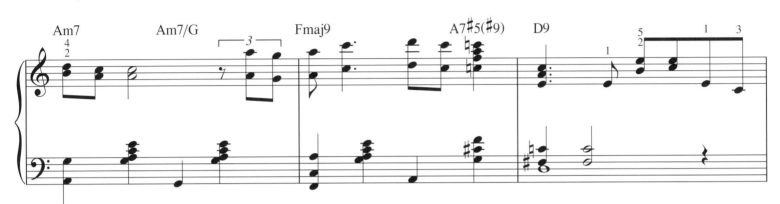

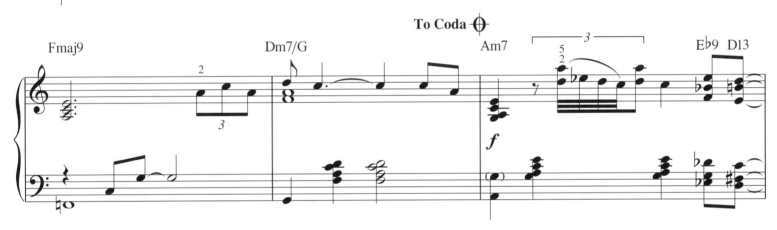

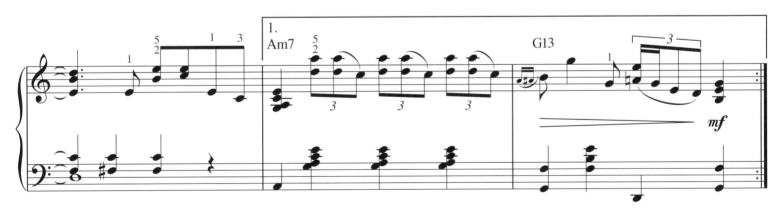

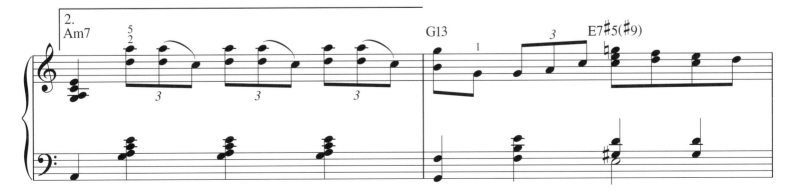

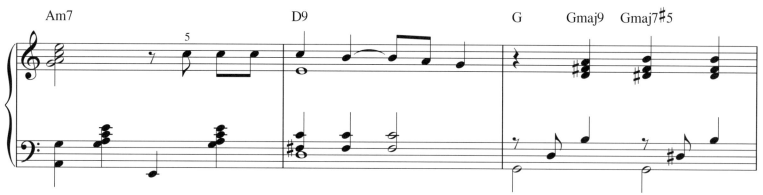

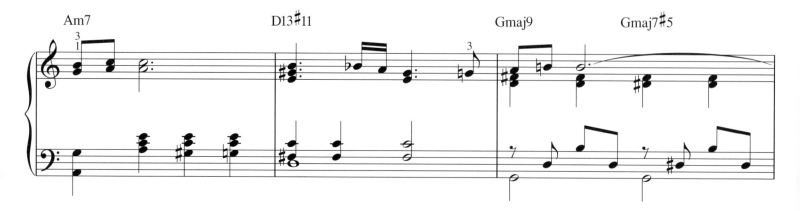

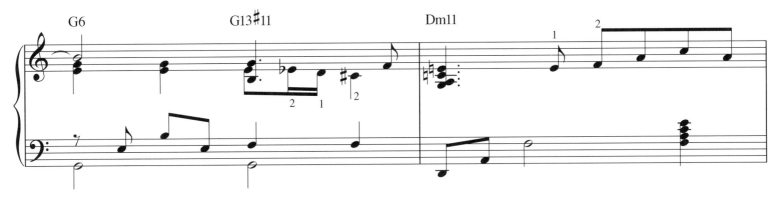

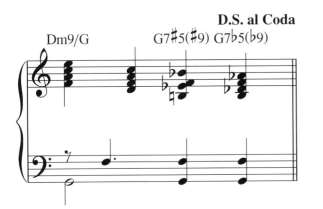

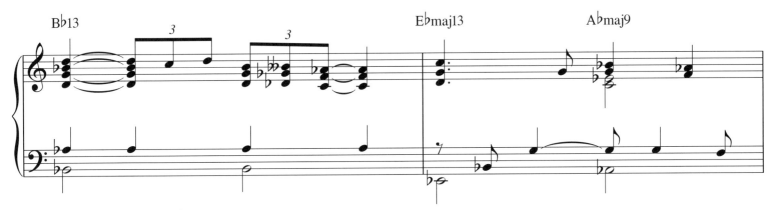

ON BROADWAY

Words and Music by BARRY MANN,
CYNTHIA WEIL, MIKE STOLLER
and JERRY LEIBER

Moderate Swing

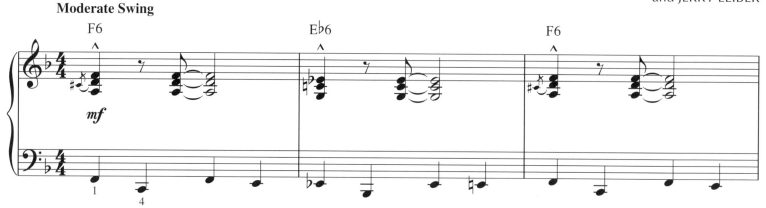

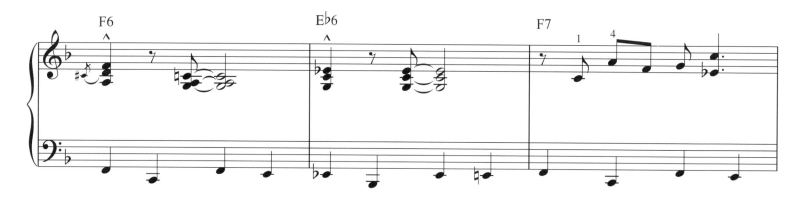

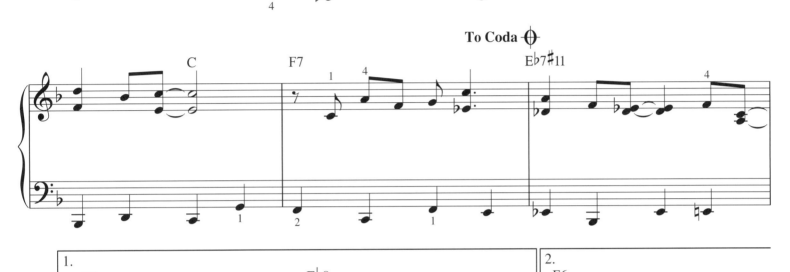

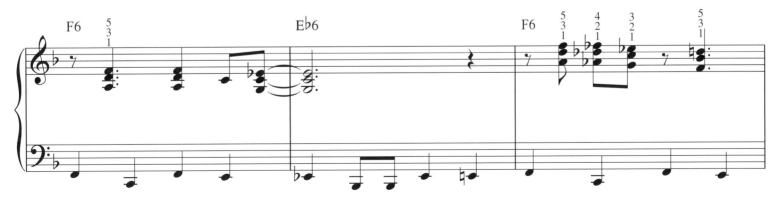

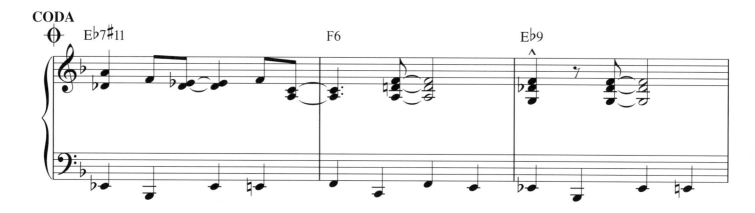

NORWEGIAN WOOD
(This Bird Has Flown)

Words and Music by JOHN LENNON
and PAUL McCARTNEY

Fast Swing Waltz

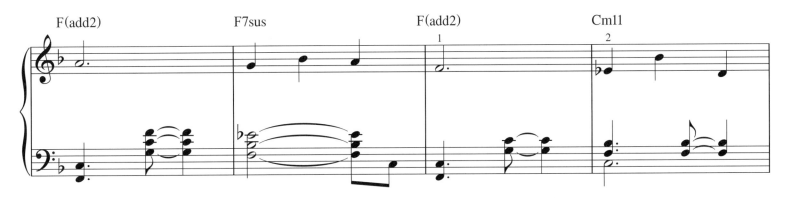

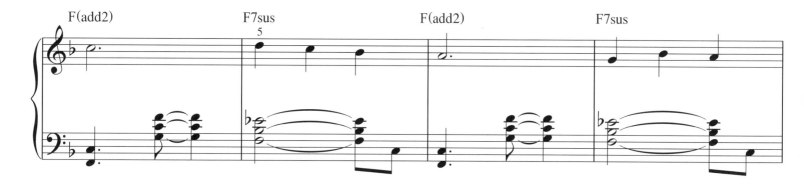

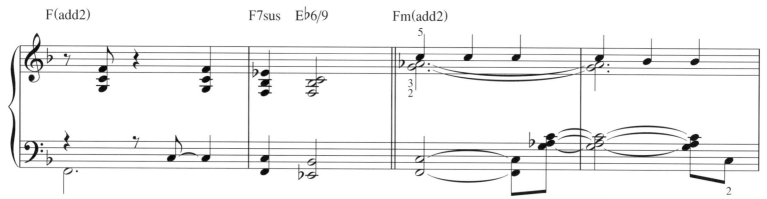

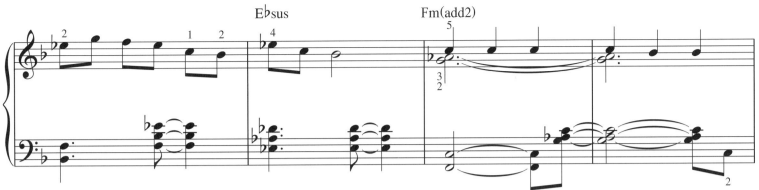

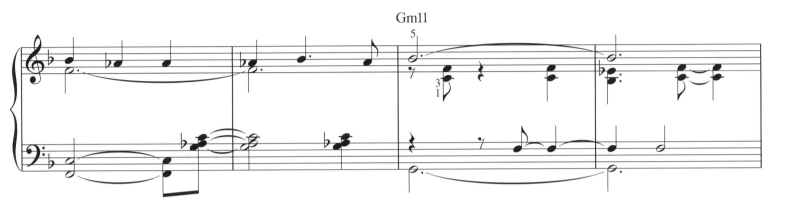

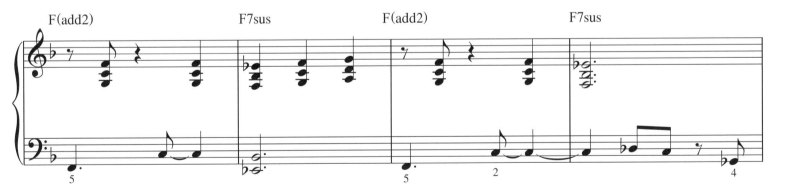

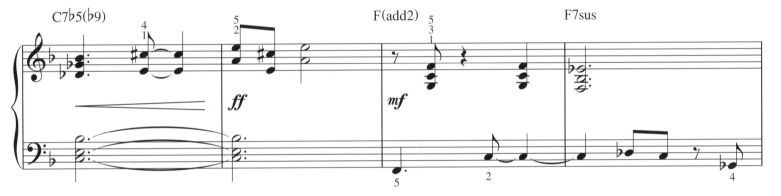

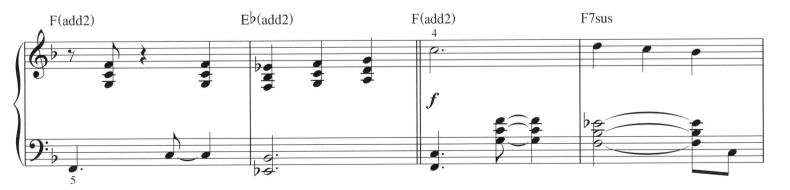

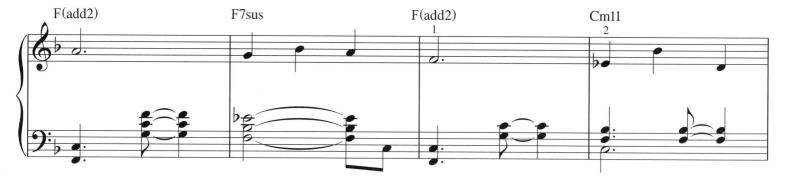

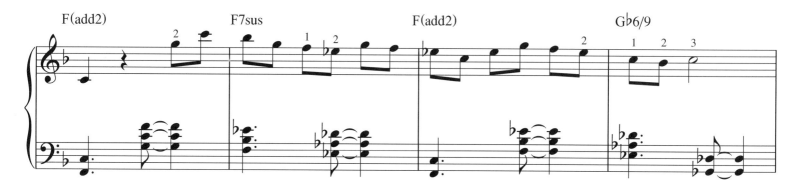

To Coda ⊕

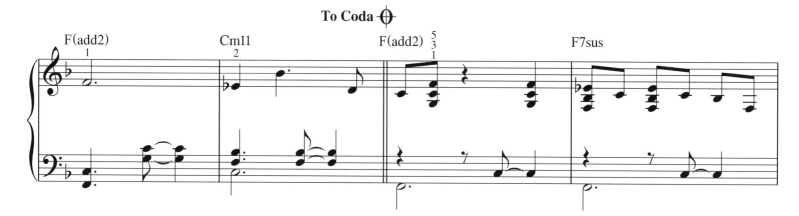

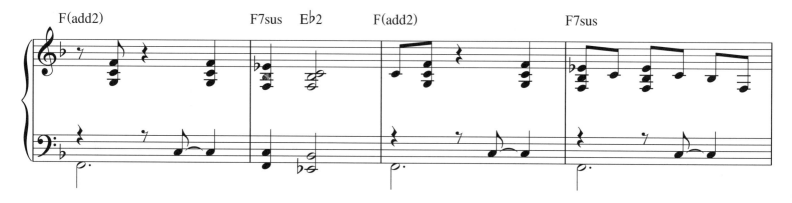

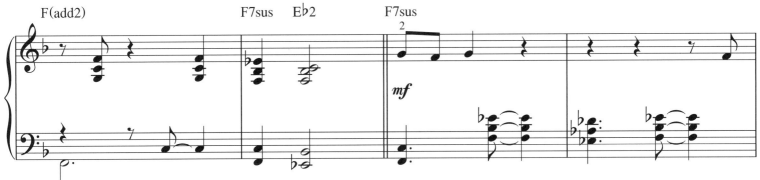

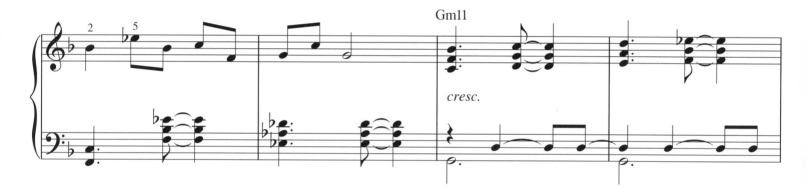

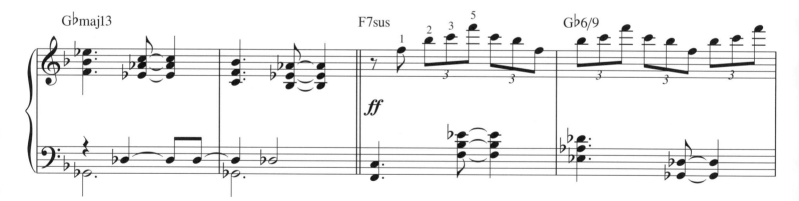

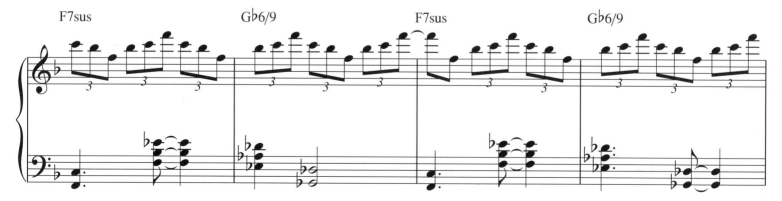

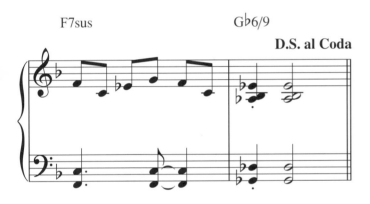

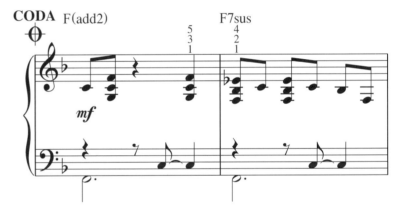

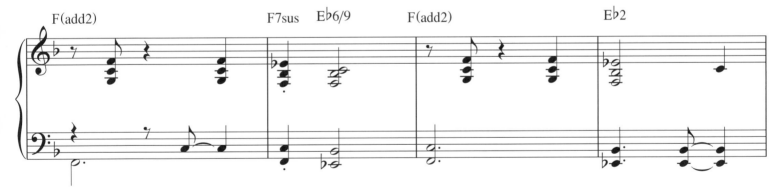

OYE COMO VA

Words and Music by
TITO PUENTE

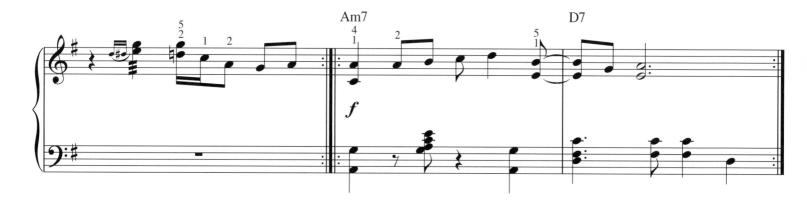

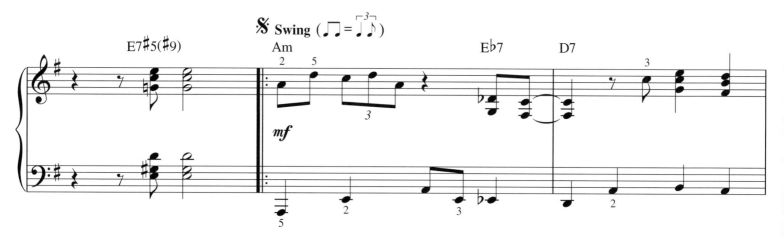

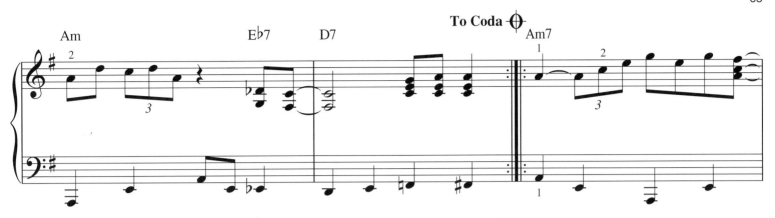

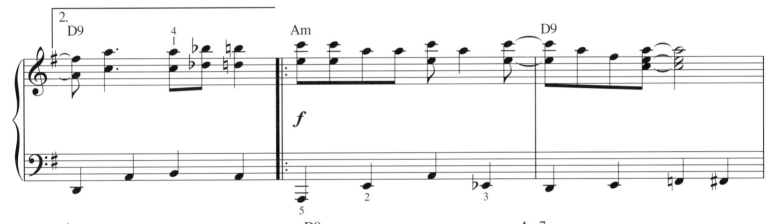

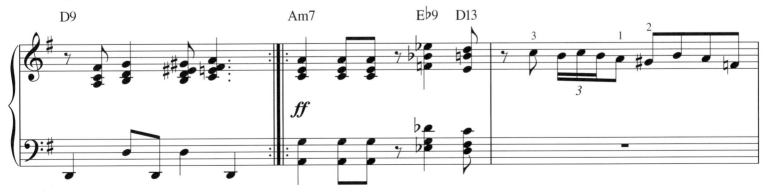

66

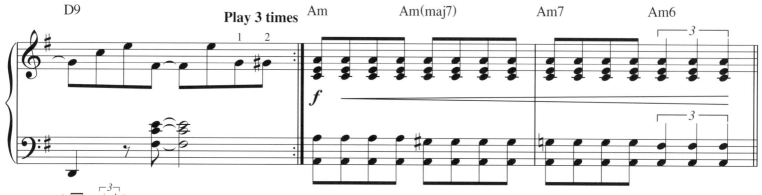

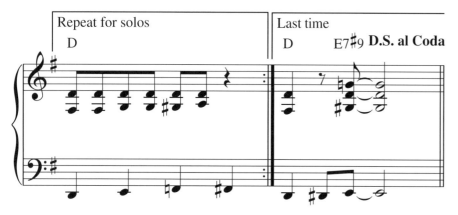

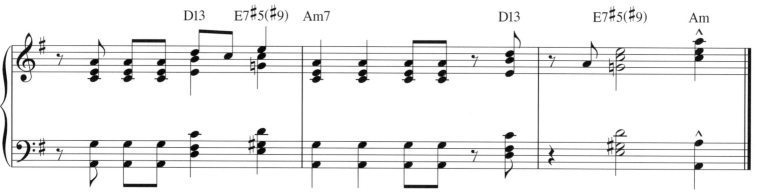

ROXANNE

Music and Lyrics by
STING

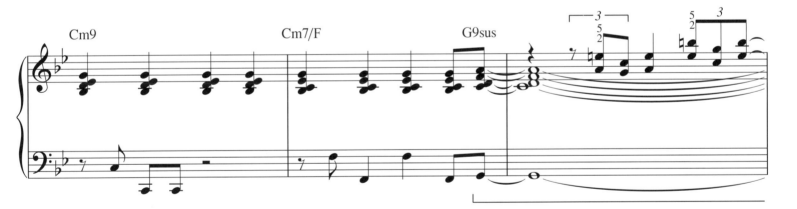

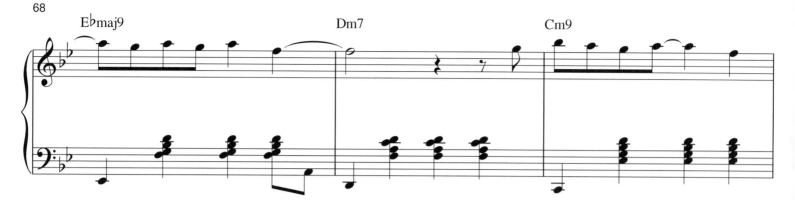

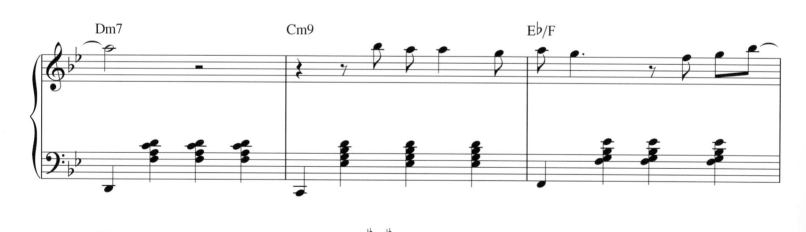

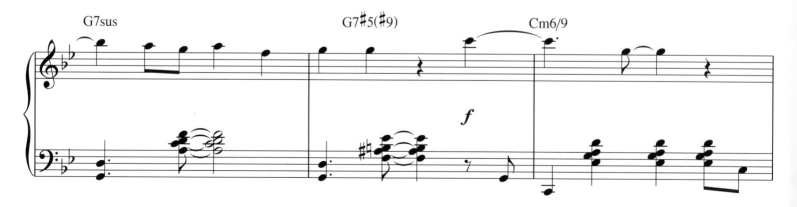

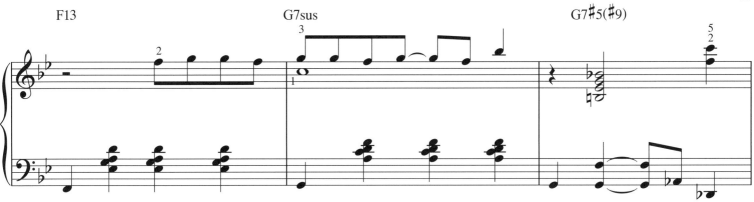

To Coda ⊕

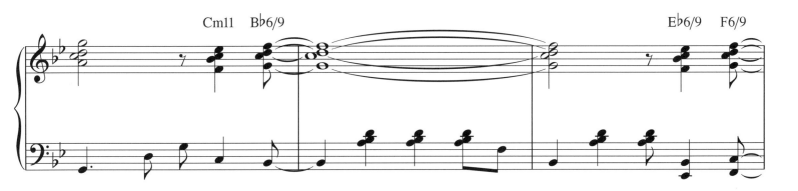

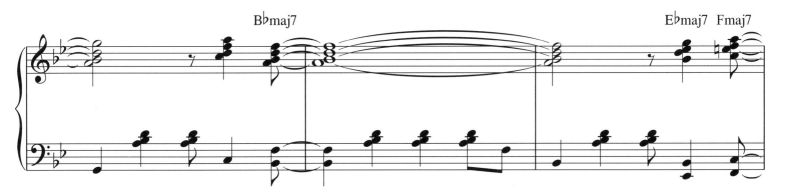

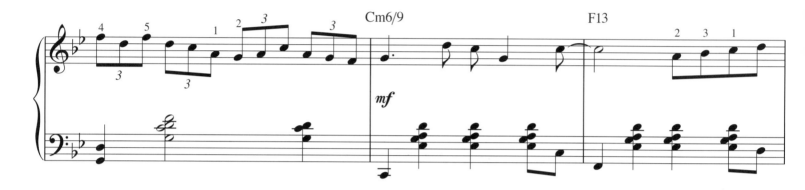

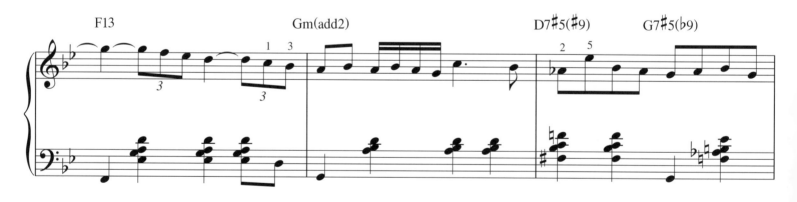

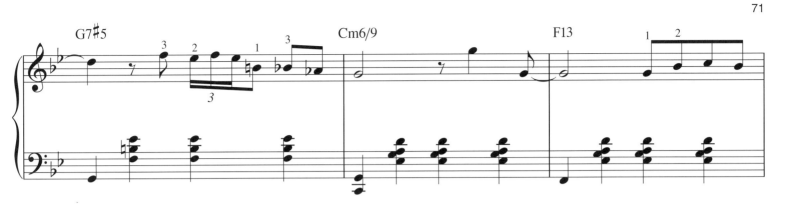

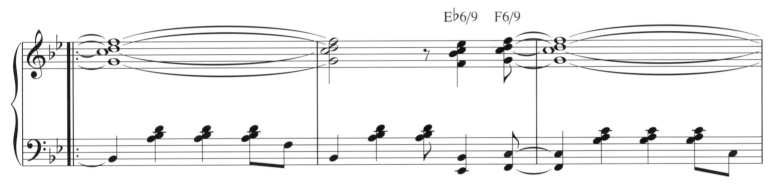

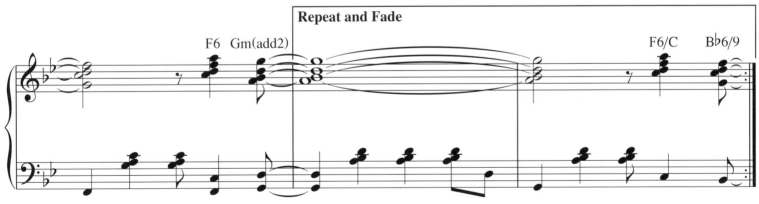

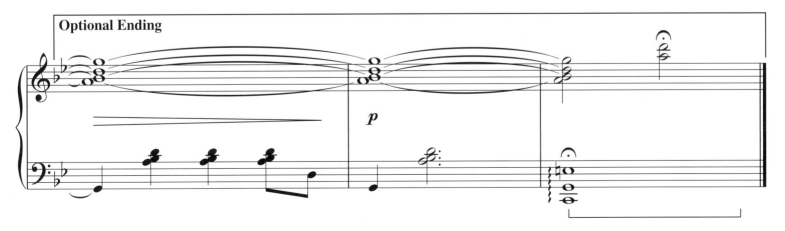

RAINY DAYS AND MONDAYS

Lyrics by PAUL WILLIAMS
Music by ROGER NICHOLS

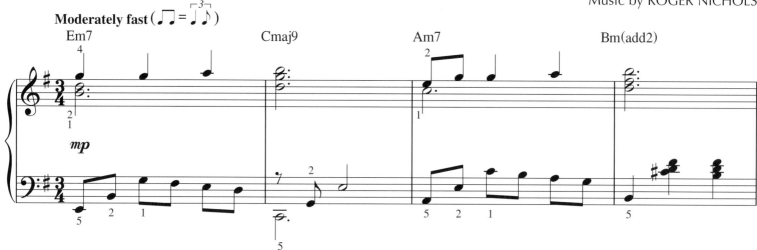

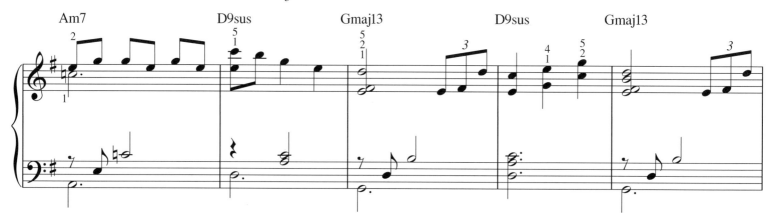

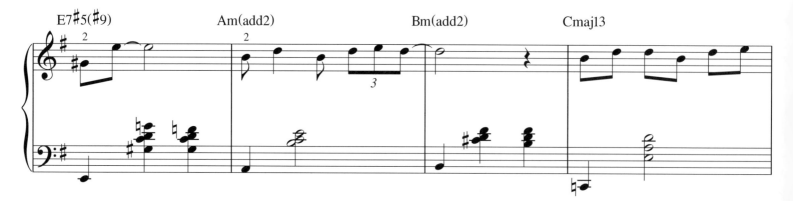

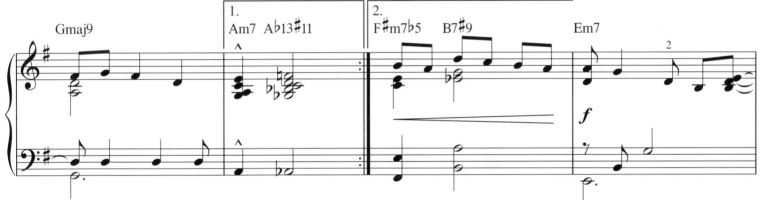

74

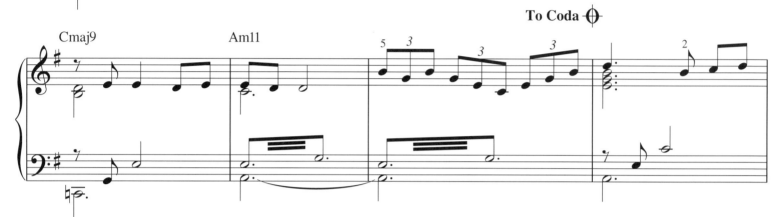

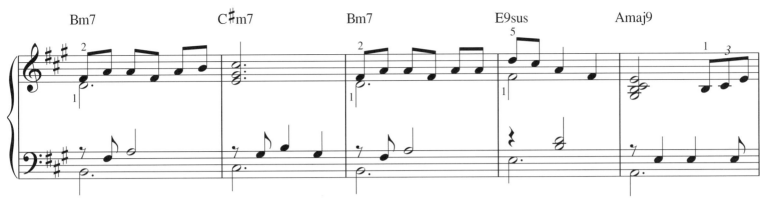

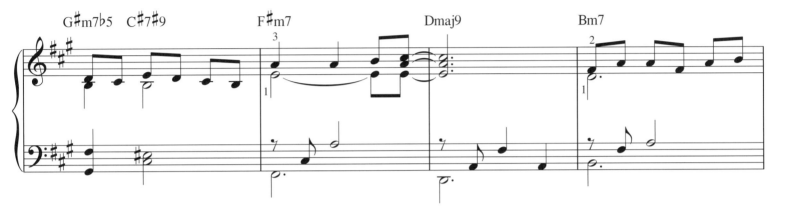

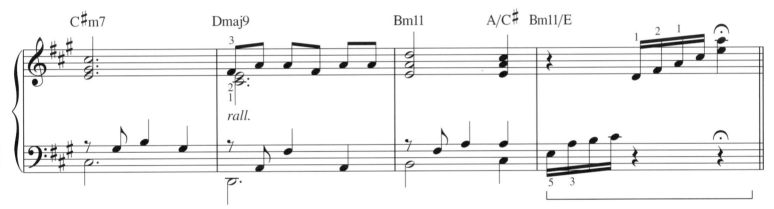

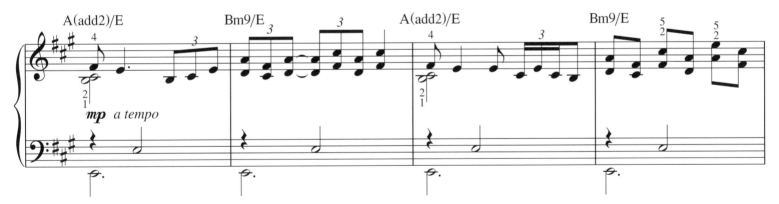

RIKKI DON'T LOSE THAT NUMBER

Words and Music by WALTER BECKER
and DONALD FAGEN

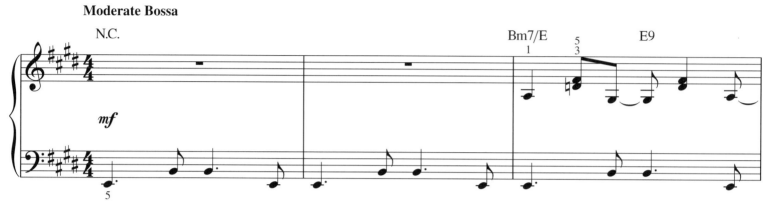

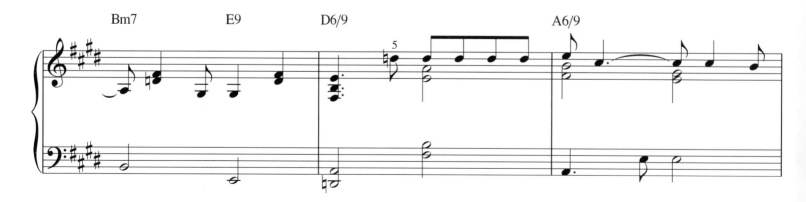

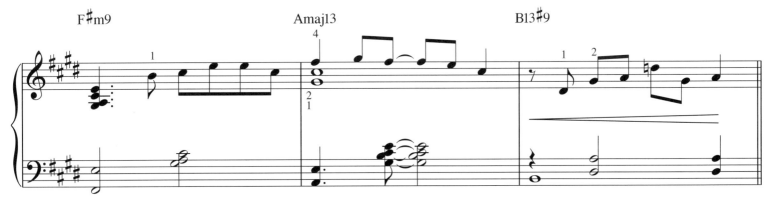

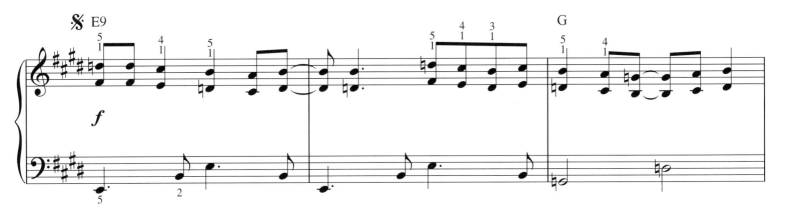

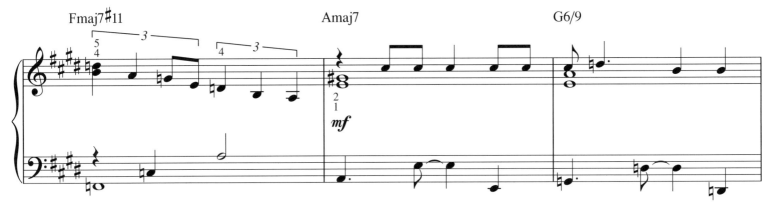

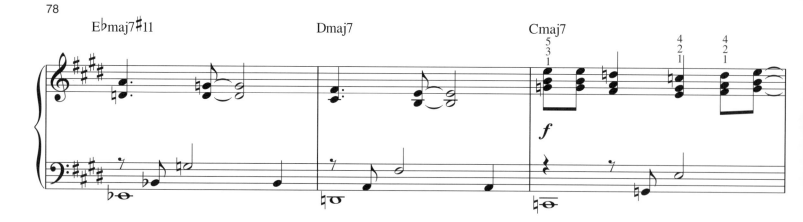

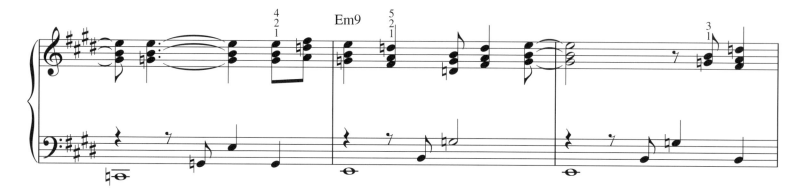

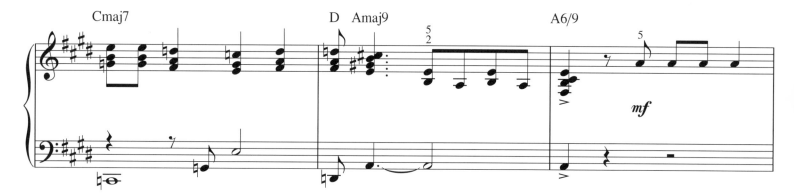

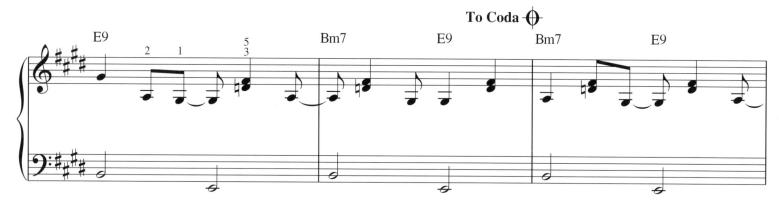

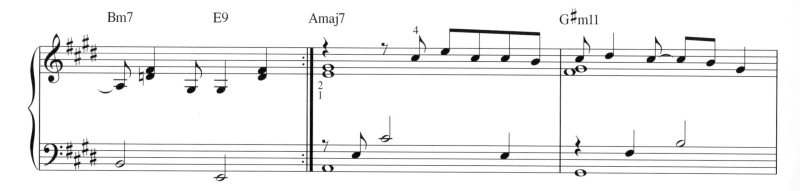

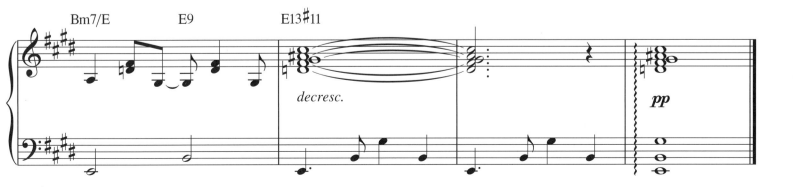

SPINNING WHEEL

Words and Music by
DAVID CLAYTON THOMAS

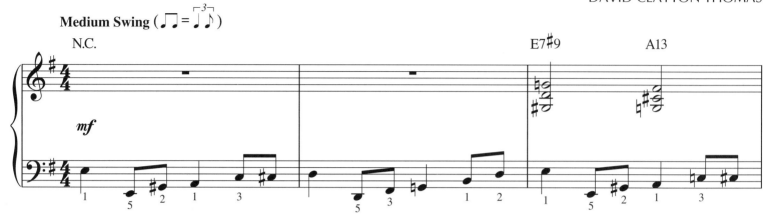

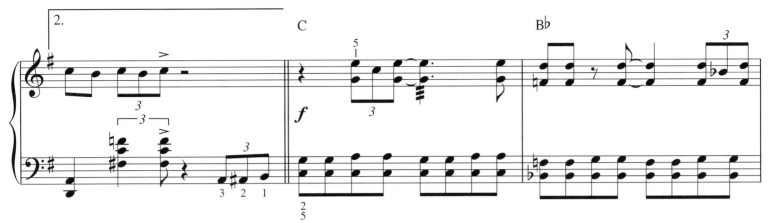

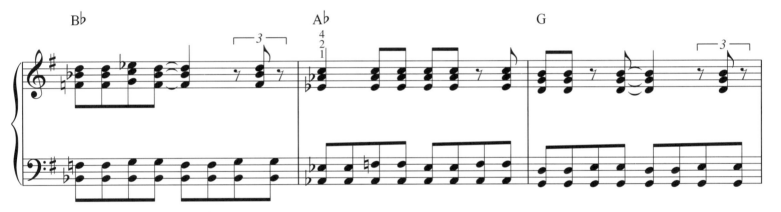

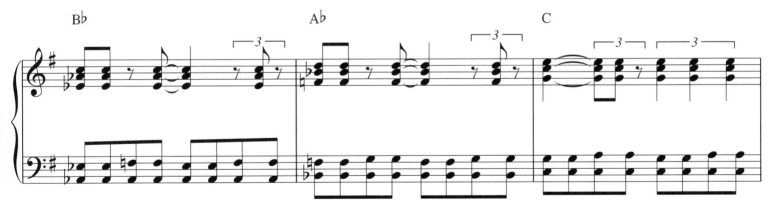

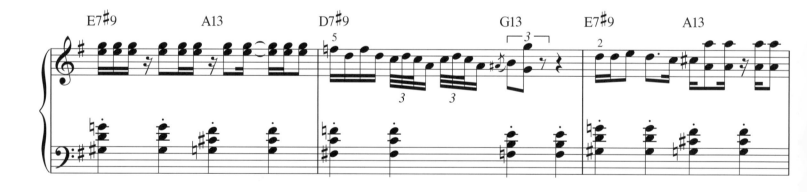

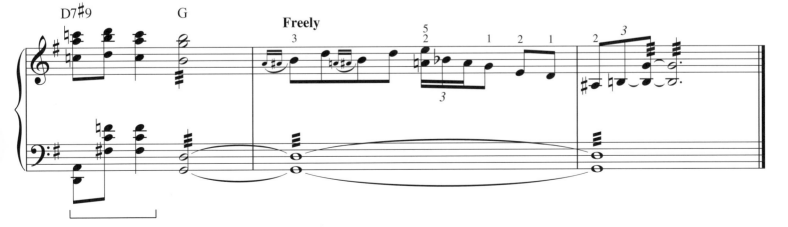

SUNNY

Words and Music by
BOBBY HEBB

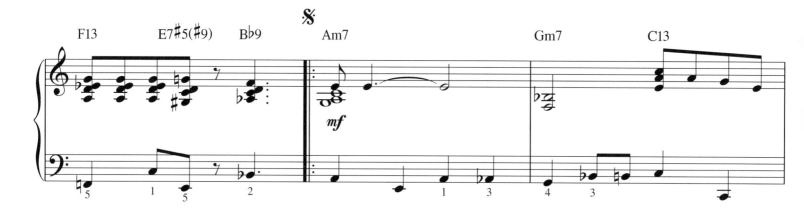

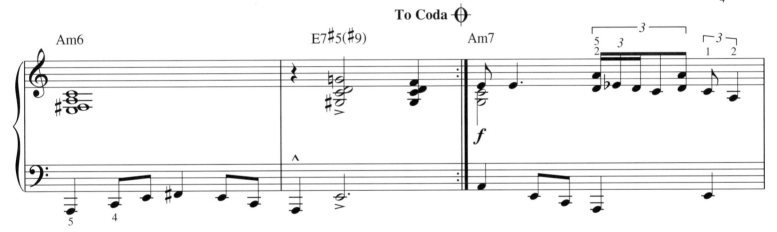

To Coda ⊕

86

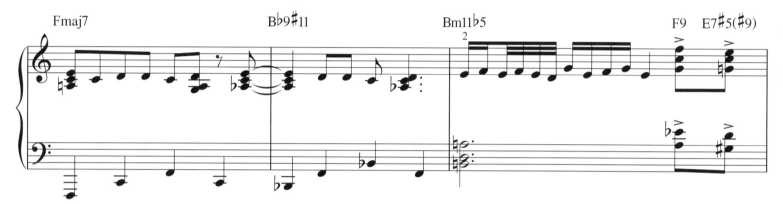

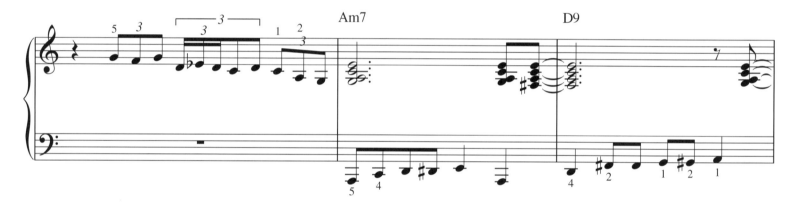

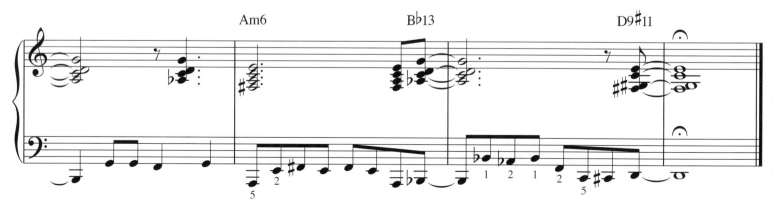

WHAT A WONDERFUL WORLD

Words and Music by GEORGE DAVID WEISS
and BOB THIELE

Slowly, with feeling

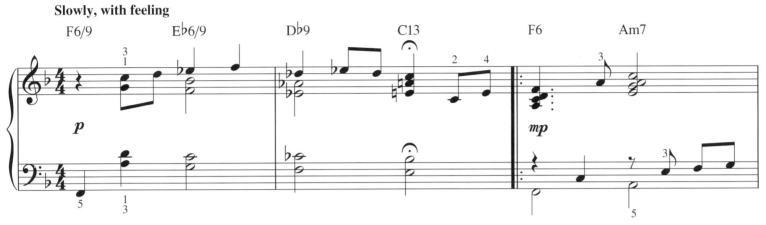

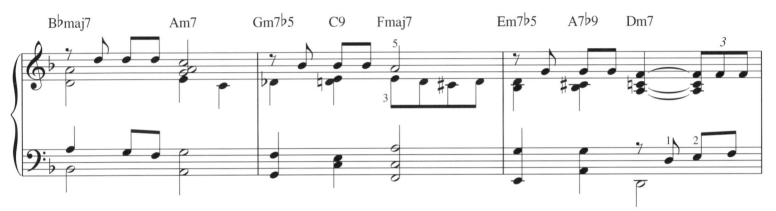

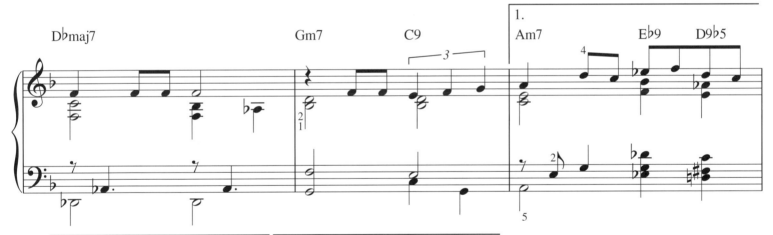

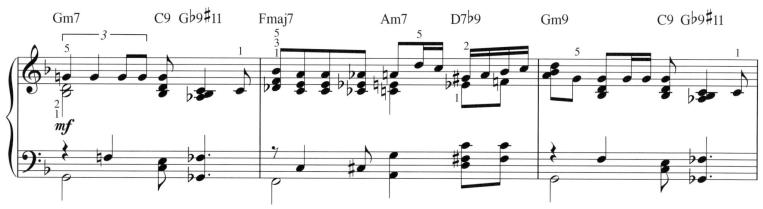

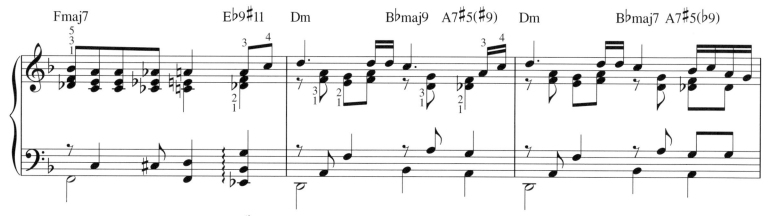

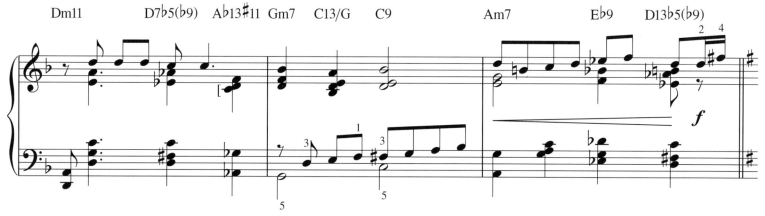

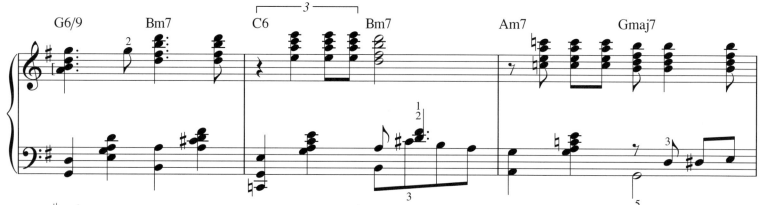

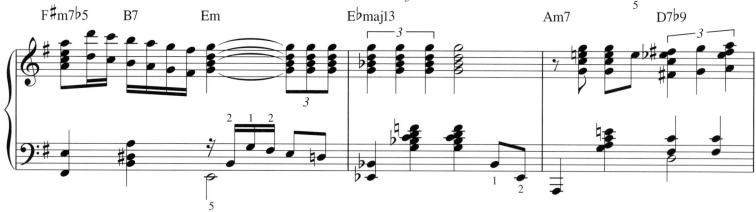

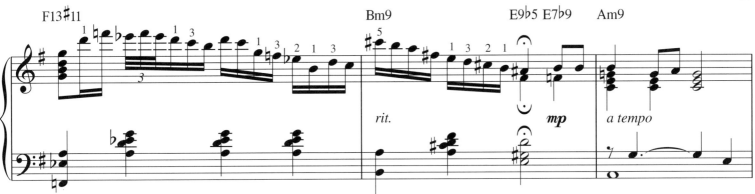

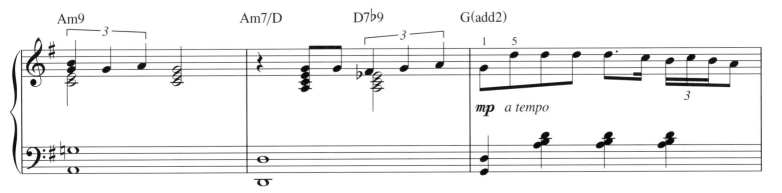

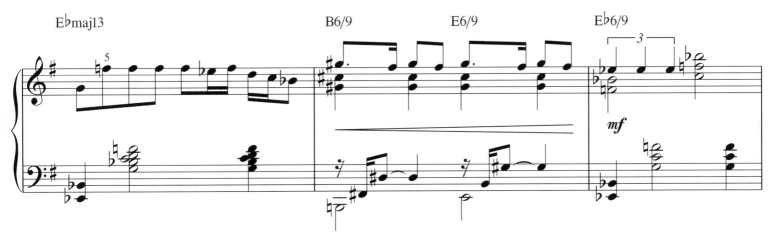

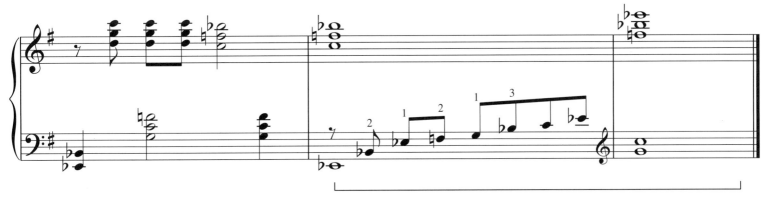

WHAT A FOOL BELIEVES

Words and Music by MICHAEL McDONALD
and KENNY LOGGINS

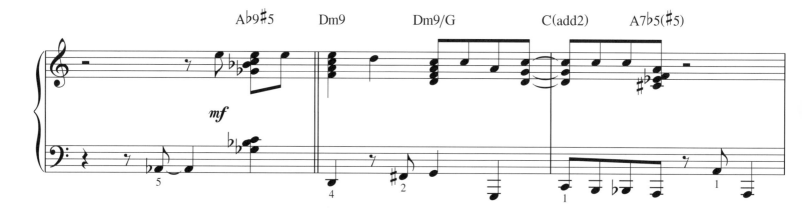

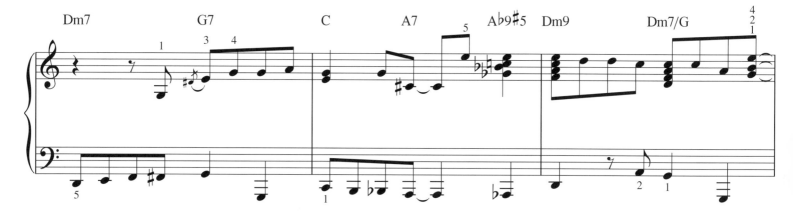

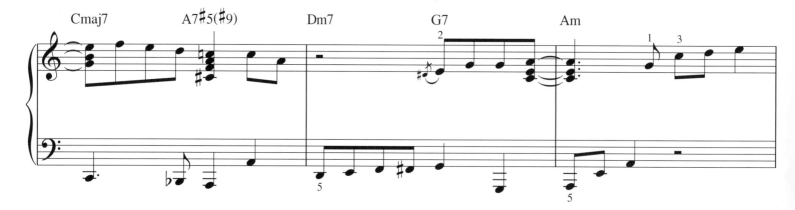

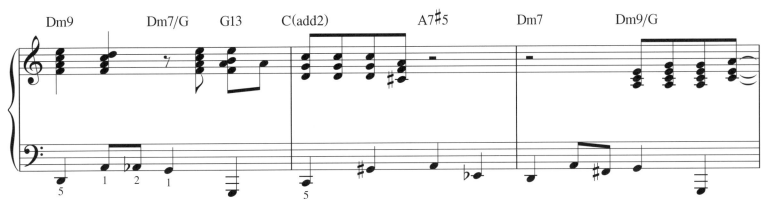

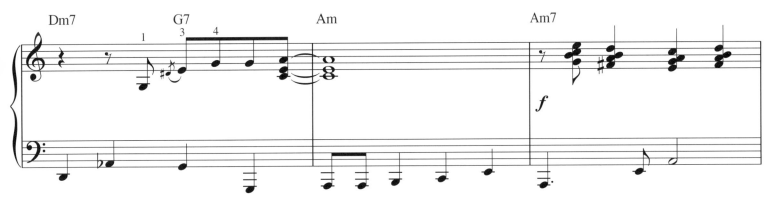

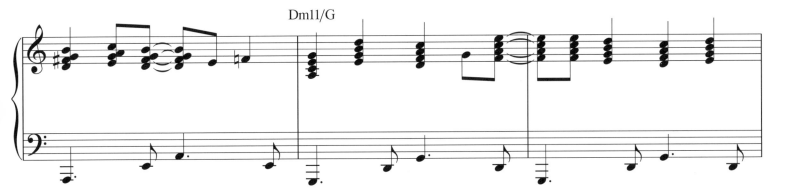

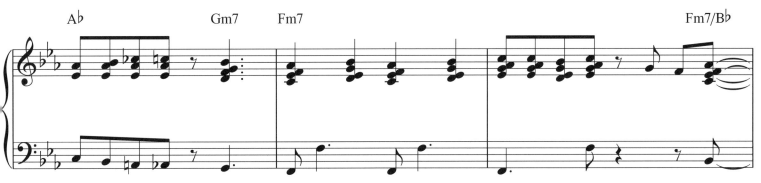

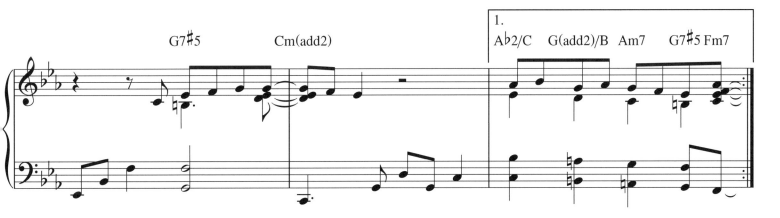

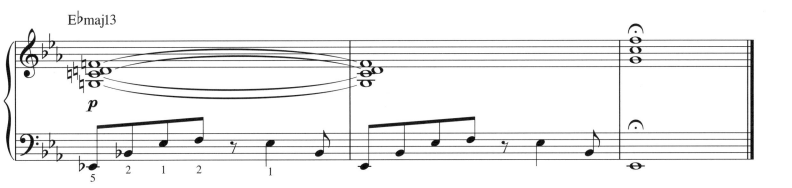

YOU ARE SO BEAUTIFUL

Words and Music by BILLY PRESTON
and BRUCE FISHER

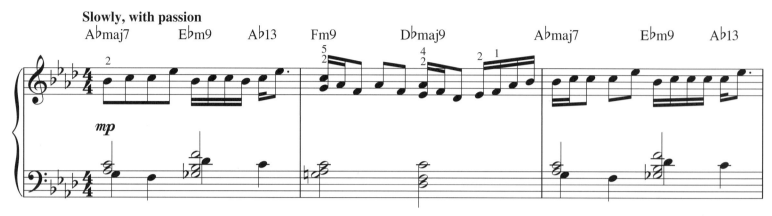

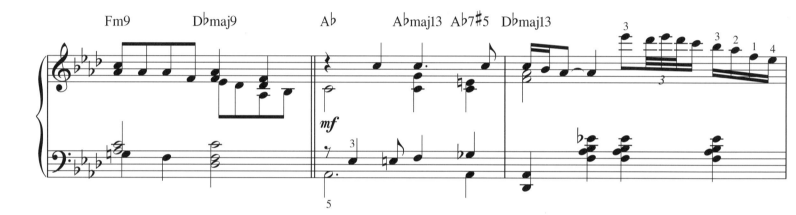

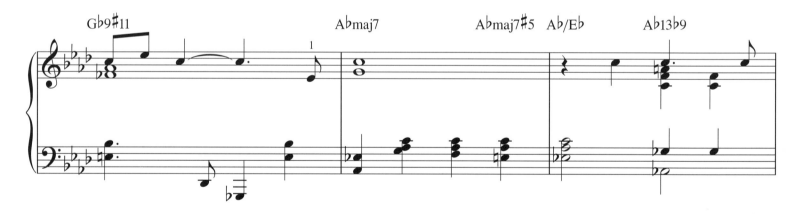

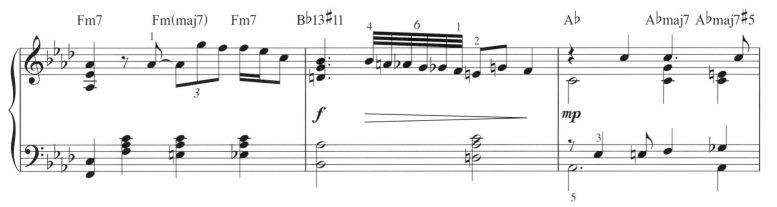

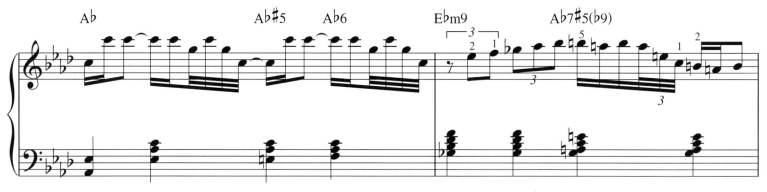

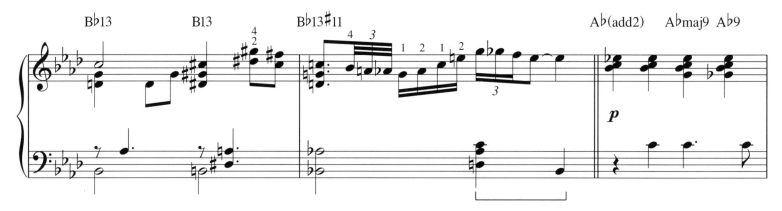

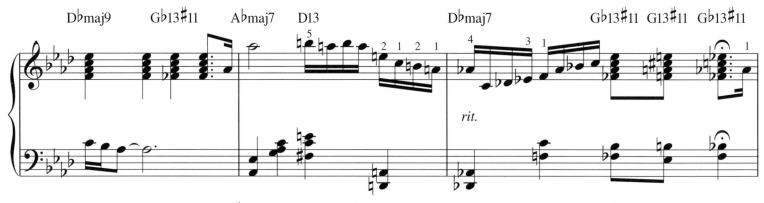

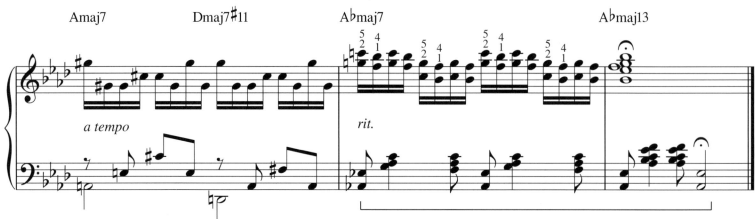